THE BIBLE'S FEASTS

LOOK FOR THESE OTHER TITLES BY DONNA BAER

In the THEOLOGY FOR NOVICES series:
The Bible's Feasts, Study Guide

The Bible's Feasts, Study Guide Leader's Edition

What the Bible Says About the Future:
Eschatology and Why it Matters in Your Life

Finding Jesus in the Old Testament

Sex and Your Soul

For parents:
Ten for Ten:
A Mother of Ten Answers the Ten Questions She's Most Frequently
Asked

Etiquette for the Twenty-first Century:
Reviving the Lovely Art of Putting Others at Ease

THE BIBLE'S FEASTS

PART OF THE
THEOLOGY FOR NOVICES SERIES

DONNA BAER

biblefeasts.com
ISBN-13:978-0615618845
ISBN-10:0615618847

Cover image: *Agnus Dei*, Francisco de Zurbarán, 1640

Bruin Publishing
Chicago, Illinois

What Great Biblical Thinkers Are Saying About Donna Baer's *The Bible's Feasts*:

"In these pages, the Feasts of Israel span the centuries, coming to life not as ancient rituals but as a framework for all of redemptive story. Written to engage the teenage mind, but also instructive for the rest of us, we discover that the feasts of Israel are rich with prophecy and present day application. Proof of this book's relevance is that Donna has taught its contents to many teenagers who, for the first time, see the Old Testament not as an ancient narrative, but a life-changing account of God's intervention into human history. Read it, learn from it and recommend it to your friends."

Dr. Erwin W. Lutzer, Senior Pastor, The Moody Church, Chicago

"Some years ago my wife and I—both Jewish believers in the Messiah—wrote a book entitled the *Fall Feasts of Israel* to try and explain these three great biblical festivals to both Christians and Jewish people. It was our hope to help the reader understand the festival and discover the fulfillment of the festivals in Jesus the Messiah. Our book was geared towards adults but it was always my hope that someone would write a book relating these magnificent truths to young people. Donna Baer has now written this book and it is my pleasure to recommend *The Bible's Feasts* to you and especially to Christian teenagers. I also believe *The Bible's Feasts* will be helpful to young people who have not yet accepted Jesus as their Messiah and are seeking spiritual solutions to the everyday challenges they face."

Dr. Mitch Glaser, President, Chosen People Ministries

"While many seek to replace the narrative of sin and redemption in the pages of scripture with a storyline that fits their own agenda, Donna has captured the redemptive meaning of the Feasts of Israel, evidencing that God's plan of salvation was always central to the life of Israel and is the source of true hope for each of us today. For those who believe the Old Testament lacks relevance for faith in the 21st century, discovering the imagery of Christ and his love for us through an understanding of the Feasts will awaken your passion for sharing the gospel. A book for all ages, make this an opportunity to deepen your understanding of Christ and his mission -- and share it with others."

Sarah Flashing, Director, The Center for Women of Faith in Culture

"Imagine the long sweep of Biblical history falling into place, making good sense, in one or two sittings with this brief book. How engaging for both teens and lifelong learners to consider the symbolic and prophetic meanings of the *Feasts—of celebrations!* — all fulfilled, and consummated, in Christ. Though I personally still hold prophetic fulfillment with questions, this thoughtful book helps us place our lives in the world's most substantial and beautiful love story—God's."

Kelly Monroe Kullberg, Founder, Veritas Forum
Finding God Beyond Harvard: the Quest for Veritas (IVP)

DEDICATION

To my knight Steve,

Who jousts for a living, and from time to time slays dragons.

From his Dulcinea.

ACKNOWLEDGMENTS

I am indebted to Erwin Lutzer and Michael Rydelnik, great preachers who are not ashamed of the gospel of Christ and who taught me to love the Torah. I am also grateful for the women of Calvary Memorial Church, who let me "try out" this material on them, and helped me to hone the message. Without Tony Buh, a good family friend and tech wizard, this project would probably have rested as a Word document indefinitely; I am most grateful to him. Finally, I want to thank my precious husband Steve, and our ten children, the apples of my eye, for their encouragement.

TABLE OF CONTENTS

INTRODUCTION

D o you enjoy stories of great treasure hunts, where clues are tucked throughout the tale, and ultimately a prize of inestimable value is revealed? The Old Testament of the Bible is such a story; from Genesis to Malachi, hints, puzzles, symbols, and road signs are imbedded to point to the treasure awaiting anyone who will look. That treasure is no mere stash of gold and jewels, but it is God Himself, King of the universe, hidden in flesh, and eager to share the riches of His Kingdom with treasure hunters.

Some of the most fascinating, engaging clues about the Treasure are found in the book of Leviticus. There, in chapter 23, God outlines for the children of Israel seven Feasts of the Lord which commemorate treasured events in their history, *and* which point to the greatest Treasure, their Messiah. The clues we find inside the Seven Feasts of the Lord describe the "career" of the Messiah— some events that have already occurred in history and others that are still in the future. As we dig to uncover the clues and learn how precisely the map points to the first part of the Messiah's career, you will become intrigued to study the clues pointing to events that are coming in the (perhaps not-too-distant) future.

HOW THE CLUES ARE ORGANIZED

There are seven Feasts of the Lord in the Old Testament. The first three, Passover, Unleavened Bread, and Firstfruits, all take place close together in the spring of the year. The fourth Feast, Weeks, arrives a little later in the spring. Then, after a long break, the fifth Feast, Trumpets, marks the beginning of fall. The festival year is finished off with the last two fall Feasts, Day of Atonement and Tabernacles.

Each of these Feasts recalls something that happened to the children of Israel as God led them from slavery in Egypt, through the harsh desert for forty years, and ultimately to freedom in a kingdom in the Promised Land. Do you remember the story?

In chapter 15 of the first book of the Bible, God makes a solemn oath to a man named Abram. (Later God changes his name to Abraham.) God promises that He will give to Abram and to his family after him a land, more offspring than they could possibly number, and a descendant who will grow up to bless every nation in the whole world. The name the Bible gives to that special descendant of Abraham who will bless the whole world is "The Messiah."

Abraham had a son named Isaac whom he loved dearly. God promised that Isaac would grow up to have children, and that a great-great-great (he didn't know how many greats) -grandchild of Isaac would be the Messiah (Genesis 17:19). God also told Abraham that some of his descendants would be strangers in a foreign land where they would be enslaved and oppressed for four hundred years (Genesis 15:13).

In order to see if Abraham believed God's promise about Isaac being the ancestor of the Messiah, God asked Abraham to sacrifice his young son (Genesis 22). Isaac hadn't yet had any children, but Abraham knew that God had promised that Isaac would. Since Abraham knew that God could be trusted, he believed that even if Isaac died, God would do a miracle to bring Isaac back to life, because God always keeps His promises. God did allow the boy to live, by providing a substitute for Isaac. Not only did that show God that Abraham believed in the Messiah, it showed *us* an important clue about the Messiah: He would be our substitute.

When Isaac grew up, he did indeed have children: twin boys named Jacob and Esau. I bet Isaac wondered which one of them would be the ancestor of the Messiah. God didn't let Isaac wonder for long; He told him that Jacob was the covenant child— the one through whom the Messiah would come. Jacob wasn't a perfect boy, in fact at times he struggled with God so much that God gave him a nickname which in Hebrew means "Struggles with God": Israel.

Now if you think Isaac spent time scratching his head wondering which of his two sons would be the ancestor of the Messiah, get a load of this: Isaac's son Jacob (Israel) had TWELVE sons, each of whom became the head of a tribe of Israel. The sons' names were: Rueben, Simeon, Levi, Judah, Issachar, Zebulon, Joseph, Benjamin, Dan, Naphtali, Gad and Asher. But God let Israel know which son would carry the special line of the Messiah: it was Judah!

I will tell you more about Judah later, but right now I have to let you know what happened to Judah's brother, Joseph. Joseph was the favorite son of his father Israel. (I know, it's not right for fathers to have favorites. I'm not saying it was right; I'm just telling you what happened.) To honor Joseph, Israel gave him a special colorful coat. Joseph at times let his special status go to his head, and would boast a bit to his brothers. (I know, that's not right either.) But what Joseph's brothers did was much worse than being boastful. They plotted to murder their brother! At the last minute, Judah changed the plan and sold his brother Joseph as a slave instead.

You might think that was the end of the story for Joseph, but God had a plan for him. At first the plan didn't seem very good. Joseph went from being a slave to being a prisoner in a dungeon. (You must really read the whole story for yourself in the first book of the Bible, chapters 37-50. It's a page-turner.) But God, through a remarkable series of events (I won't spoil the story by telling you all the details— you really must read it!), brought Joseph out of the dungeon, and placed him as second-in-command of the most powerful nation on the earth at the time, Egypt. There Joseph was, walking around the pyramids, and the Great Sphinx and the Nile— more important than anyone but Pharaoh!

God revealed to Joseph that in seven years, all throughout the land of Egypt and in all the surrounding lands, there was going to be a LONG famine. Joseph convinced Pharaoh to store up grain so that when the famine came, they would not starve in Egypt. Through another series of extra-ordinary events, Joseph's brothers, those no-good-nicks, came begging for food in Egypt. Joseph, forgiving his brothers (who, to be fair, had grown to regret their sinfulness), urged them to come to Egypt to live, since the famine was going to last a long time.

And so, all the children of Israel moved from Canaan to Egypt, seventy of them in all. At first, they were treated well— after all, Uncle Joseph was the number two man in the most powerful nation in the world. Years later, when Joseph was about to die, he made all the children of Israel solemnly promise that when they left Egypt and returned to the land of Canaan, as God had promised Abraham, that they would take his mummified body with them.

Alas, Joseph did die, and after a few decades, new Pharaohs came along who did not remember how Joseph had saved the nation of Egypt.

They began to treat the children of Israel cruelly, and turned them into slaves. As the years went by, their slavery became intolerable. Throughout their travails, Joseph's mummy remained in their midst as a constant reminder that God would not abandon his children in Egypt forever. After 400 years of captivity, the children of Israel cried out to the Lord to send them someone to deliver them from their oppressors.

God, who had promised Abraham that after 400 years of slavery He would deliver the Israelites, kept His promise by sending a man named Moses. Moses, like Joseph, had risen from slavery to a very high rank in Egypt. Moses fell from Pharaoh's favor, but was found in God's favor. God sent him to Pharaoh to demand the release of God's covenant people, now numbering over a million, from slavery. Pharaoh initially refused. So God sent a plague, and Pharaoh relented. But Pharaoh changed his mind. So God sent another plague, and Pharaoh relented. But Pharaoh changed his mind again. So God sent a plague, over and over again— for nine times! Finally, God said, "I will bring one more plague on Pharaoh and on Egypt. After that, he will let you go from here, and when he does, he will drive you out completely (Exodus 11:1)."

Now get ready, for this is where the trail of clues found in the Feasts begins. Are you ready to hunt for a Treasure?

PART ONE:

THE SPRING FEASTS

THE FIRST FEAST: PASSOVER

"Christ our Passover has been sacrificed for us; therefore, let us keep the feast (I Corinthians 5:7)."

HOW GOD SAVED HIS PEOPLE IN EGYPT

The last plague that God was about to send was a plague of death—for all the firstborn in the land. At midnight on Nisan 15 (that's how you name dates in the Bible— it's in our springtime) the Lord was going to strike EVERY household. Every family. Every home. UNLESS...

God provided ONE way to be saved from the judgment. He said that if His children would take a perfect male lamb, kill it without breaking any of its bones, and put the blood of the lamb over the doorframes of their homes, He would see the blood and pass over the house. The blood of the lamb of God would save the people.

If anyone in Egypt had thought he could be saved from judgment by any means except the blood, that night he would hold the limp body of a dead boy in his arms. Being nice couldn't save them. Giving money to the poor couldn't save them. The gods of Egypt couldn't save them. Only the blood could save them.

That night the angel of the Lord went through the land, and all those who trusted in the blood of lamb of God were saved. In every household where they did not believe God, there was death. The firstborn of the prisoner: dead. The firstborn of all the livestock: dead. The firstborn of Pharaoh: dead.

God told the children of Israel to remember the night He spared them in passing over them, by having a Feast, a special religious remembrance, every year. He told them to call the feast Passover. By keeping the Passover, the children of Israel would always remember that God saved them by the blood of the lamb. Year in and year out, a Hebrew would say to himself, "God saved us by the blood of the lamb."

**But God didn't institute the Feast
just to remind His people of what He did;
He wanted to let His children know what He was going to do.**

THE LAMB OF GOD

When we first meet Jesus in the New Testament book of John, John the Baptist says something that sounds kind of funny to us, but was full of meaning to a Jewish person living in Judea in the first century. John saw Jesus coming toward him and said, "Behold the Lamb of God who takes away the sin of the world (John 1:29b)."

Jewish people who heard Jesus being called the Lamb of God, would think immediately of the Passover lamb, whose blood took away the judgment that was on all the land. They would think of that flawless male that was sacrificed without breaking its bones, in order to save them.

Jesus went on to live among the people of Judea and Samaria, perfectly keeping every law of God. He never lied. He never disrespected His parents. He never harbored an impure thought. He was flawless, just like the Passover lamb. For three years He lived openly among the people of that land and never once broke a rule, or failed to keep a commandment.

At the end of those three years, Jesus, the flawless, male, Lamb of God, joined His friends in Jerusalem during the month of Nisan for the dinner that all Jews were commanded to eat. It was the Passover dinner. As I mentioned, the Jewish calendar is different from ours, and there were even slightly different versions of the calendar among different Jewish groups. Consequently, some Jews in Jerusalem were celebrating the Passover on Thursday evening; others would celebrate it on Friday.

JESUS' LAST PASSOVER

On that Thursday Passover, Jesus told His friends that He had eagerly desired to eat this meal with them. This wasn't going to be just an ordinary Passover dinner. This was going to be the LAST Passover supper that would ever point to what God would do in the future. The time had arrived when Jesus would do the things that the Passover had been pointing to for nearly 1,500 years. After this Passover, the people of God would no longer think back to a furry little lamb whose blood elicited God's mercy, saved them, and freed them from slavery; believers would forevermore think of Jesus, the Lamb of God whose blood satisfied God's wrath, saved them from judgment, and freed them from bondage to sin.

A Passover dinner, both in Jesus' day and in ours, includes four glasses of wine. The third glass has always been called the Cup of Redemption. The word "redemption," in the old days, had a definition we don't use much today. It meant, "the ransom paid to buy a slave's freedom." For 1500 years, those who were waiting for the Messiah would hold up the Cup of Redemption on the evening of Passover, and remember the lamb of God who suffered to purchase their redemption— their freedom from slavery.

During Jesus' last Passover, His Last Supper, He held up the Cup of Redemption and He gave His friends some startling news: "This cup is the covenant in *My* blood." You see, the redemption cup was all along pointing to the blood of the promised Messiah, the Lamb of God— Jesus. The red wine in the redemption cup pointed to Jesus' blood that would pay the ransom to buy the children He loved from their slavery to sin.

When the Passover Supper— Jesus' Last Supper— had ended, Jesus left with His friends to go to the Mount of Olives. There He was betrayed by His friend Judas, and turned over to the religious leaders who were trying to kill Him. They persuaded the Roman government to execute Him.

At nine o'clock on Friday morning, Jesus was nailed to a cruel Roman cross, with a criminal crucified on either side of Him. The nineteenth chapter of the book of John tells us that though the bones of the criminals were broken during their executions, not one of Jesus' bones was broken. (There was also a prophecy about this in Psalm 34. Look it up; it's cool.) Finally, at three o'clock, the very hour that many of the Jews in Jerusalem were sacrificing their unblemished, unbroken Passover lambs, Jesus, the unblemished, unbroken Lamb of God, was sacrificed for our sins.

The Bible tells us that everyone on earth sins. We tell lies, we don't obey our parents, we are unkind to our brothers and sisters. God in His Word tells us that these sins deserve a punishment. And since the one we've disobeyed when we sin is the God who created the whole universe and everything in it, the punishment has to be huge. (The person you sin against *does* make a difference in determining your punishment. If you hit your brother, you might get grounded. If you hit the President of the United States, you'd be thrown in jail!) In fact, since the One whom we violate in our rebellion is eternal— never having a beginning or an ending, our punishment needs to match; it needs to be eternal. And it is. The Bible tells us that the punishment for sin is to be eternally separated from God. The only way we could possibly get out of our eternal punishment is if someone eternal suffered it for us. And that was Jesus.

The first chapter of the book of John tells us that Jesus was alive forever with God, even before He got a body and was born in the stable in Bethlehem. And it tells us that He is going to live forever and ever into the future. Jesus, the eternal Son of God became the Lamb of God to pay our eternal debt in our place. His death could be substituted for ours, and His sacrifice was sufficient to pay our eternal debt, because He was eternal. And He paid our eternal debt on the Feast of Passover.

The last thing Jesus said as He hung on the cross on the Feast of Passover was the Greek word, "Tetelestai (John 19:30)." This was normally the term written across a loan document when it was paid in full, to indicate that the whole debt was paid, and nothing more was owed. On that Passover, the eternal Lamb of God paid the eternal debt we owed— our redemption price. And He paid it in full. He did it all. Tetelestai.

To remind believers that Jesus Christ, the Lamb of God, had finished all the work that was required to save them, the Bible says, "Christ our Passover has been sacrificed for us (I Corinthians 5:7)." The Passover lamb in Egypt was sacrificed once, and His blood was all that was needed to save the people. Christ our Passover was sacrificed once, and His blood is all that we need to save us.

How was it that an Israelite living in bondage in Egypt was saved from death? He placed his faith in God's provision through the blood. How is it that you or I can be saved from the eternal debt that we owe

God? We place our trust in God's provision in the blood of the eternal Lamb of God. The Bible tells us, "Believe in the Lord Jesus, and you will be saved (Acts 16:31)." In the land of Egypt, the blood of the lamb did all the work. In your land, the blood of Jesus, the Lamb of God, did all the work. And He did it on the Feast of Passover.

Who, in his wildest imagination,
would have dreamed that the event
to which the Feast had pointed,
year after year, century after century,
would have occurred on the actual day of the Feast?

HOW ABOUT YOU?

ARE YOU TRUSTING IN THE FINISHED WORK OF THE LAMB OF GOD, JESUS? IN THE LAND OF EGYPT, A FIRSTBORN WHO TRUSTED IN ANYTHING OTHER THAN THE BLOOD OF THE LAMB OF GOD PERISHED. HIS GOOD WORKS COULDN'T SAVE HIM. HIS GENEROSITY COULDN'T SAVE HIM. AND CERTAINLY THE GODS OF EGYPT COULDN'T SAVE HIM. THERE IS ONLY ONE TRUE GOD, AND HE IS MIGHTY TO SAVE. IF YOU HAVEN'T PLACED YOUR TRUST IN JESUS, THE LAMB OF GOD, DO IT RIGHT NOW, EVEN BEFORE YOU READ THE NEXT CHAPTER. IF YOU NEED HELP THINKING OF WORDS TO SAY ALOUD TO HIM, YOU COULD SAY SOMETHING LIKE, "LORD JESUS, I KNOW THAT YOU ARE PERFECT AND SINLESS, AND THAT YOU HAVE ALREADY PAID THE ETERNAL DEBT THAT I OWE BECAUSE OF MY SIN. I TRUST IN YOU NOW, AND BELIEVE THAT THE BLOOD YOU SHED ON THE CROSS PAID MY DEBT IN FULL. THANK YOU FOR BEING MY SUBSTITUTE, FOR TAKING MY PLACE SO THAT I DON'T HAVE TO SPEND ETERNITY SEPARATED FROM YOU. THANK YOU FOR PASSING OVER ME IN JUDGMENT. I AM YOURS."

THE SECOND FEAST:

UNLEAVENED BREAD

"So if the Son has set you free, you will be free indeed (John 8:36)."

GOD FREES HIS CHILDREN

When God freed His children from the shackles of slavery, He told them to leave the land of Egypt quickly. God knew that after the tenth plague, Pharaoh would finally relent and grant the Hebrews their freedom. But He also knew that Pharaoh would quickly regret his decision, and try to make the Hebrews his slaves once again. If the people did not walk quickly in the freedom God had provided, then Egypt would become their grave.

God also knew that when someone has been a slave for a long time, he is often reluctant to embrace freedom, even when it is purchased for him. A person accustomed to the bondage of slavery is sometimes inclined to rot and decay as a captive rather than boldly to walk in freedom.

For example, during the American Civil War, over 618,000 men gave their lives to end slavery in the United States. When the 13th Amendment to the Constitution was signed, slavery was outlawed in the land. Yet, some former slaves continued to live in submission to their slave masters, enduring misery, even though their freedom had been purchased with blood.

Slavery is a cruel institution that robs an individual of everything he possesses, even his will to live in freedom. Knowing this, God commanded His children to leave at once— giving them no opportunity to harbor any thought of remaining captives, and denying Pharaoh the opportunity to claim what didn't belong to him. The Hebrews were to embrace their freedom *immediately*. They obeyed. As the Hebrews scrambled away, the Egyptians, now fearing the God of their former-slaves, showered them with gifts of gold. The children of Israel left Egypt in such haste that they didn't have time even to let their bread dough rise before baking it!

UNLEAVENED BREAD

If you've never baked a loaf of bread, you might not know what I'm talking about. When you make homemade bread, you first combine warm water, a little sugar and some yeast (which is also called leaven). Yeast is actually a fungus that is activated in warm water, and feeds on sugar. As the yeast feeds, its waste product is methane gas. When you add flour to the yeast mixture, the "yeast gas" expands the dough so that after a few hours it becomes big and puffy. Usually, you punch down the dough and let it rise again for another few hours before you bake it for an hour. Then, at long last, you pull a huge fluffy loaf from the oven. If for some reason you forget to add the yeast (as I did once in my bread machine), after several hours you pull a small, dense rock out of the oven!

When God redeemed His children, He instructed them to take hold of their freedom quickly— so quickly that the yeast in the bread they were making didn't have time to get to work. To commemorate the fact that God did not abandon His people to the graves of Egypt, nor did He allow them to wallow and decay in slavery, He instituted the Feast of Unleavened Bread. This second Feast in the Jewish calendar begins the day after the Feast of Passover, and lasts seven days. (Sometimes in the Bible, the first three Feasts of the year are lumped together and are collectively called "The Feast of Unleavened Bread," in the same way that we might call Christmas Eve, Christmas Day and New Year's Day "The Christmas Holidays.")

On the first day of the Feast of Unleavened Bread, those who were waiting for the Messiah were instructed to remove all the leaven from their homes, and from the entire community. Then, for the seven days following, no one was allowed to eat anything with leaven in it. (It's worse than you think. Leaven isn't in bread only; it's in cake and pizza crust and cookies. No goodies for a week.) If anyone broke the

Feast and ate something with leaven in it, he was thrown out of the community!

When a Hebrew mother would painstakingly clean crumbs out of every nook of her home, or when a Hebrew father would burn all the bread that he had labored to buy, or when a Hebrew child would abstain from baked treats for a week, each would think back to that time when God liberated them from their captivity and instructed them to live as free men. They would remember that with His outstretched arm, God did all the work necessary to make them free, and all they had to do was to walk in the liberty purchased for them. God loved them so much that He did not abandon them to the graves of Egypt, nor did He let His chosen ones decay in bondage.

**But God didn't institute the Feast
just to remind His people of what He did;
He wanted to let His children know what He was going to do.**

LEAVEN AND SIN

To get some hints about what God was going to do on the Feast, we must turn to the New Testament of the Bible, where the clues come from Jesus Himself. Jesus told His friends, "Be on your guard against the yeast of the Pharisees (Luke 12:1)." Cleary, we know Jesus wasn't warning folks not to go to a Pharisee bakery. He was using the word "yeast" to symbolize something else, the way you might say, "Watch out for the venom coming out of her mouth!" (You don't really mean that your friend is a rattlesnake.) And what did Jesus use the word "yeast" to symbolize? He tells us in the same passage: hypocrisy. When Jesus said, "yeast," He was talking about a kind of sin. Regularly in the Bible, yeast is a picture of sin.

To figure out why He might have chosen yeast to stand for sin, think back to my description of making a loaf of bread. The yeast produces a gas (the same kind that you produce, by the way!) that puffs up the loaf. And sin is like that; it arrogantly puffs you up so that you think God's rules don't apply to you. That was God's enemy the devil's enormous error; he was so puffed up that he believed that he was as great as God. (Big mistake.)

Yeast also makes the loaf look beautiful...at first. My poor pitiful yeast-free loaf was surely ugly to look at, but my yeast-filled ones are so handsome they would make your mouth water. Yeast makes bread enticing and inviting— just like sin.

When other people are involved in immoral behavior, it often looks very attractive. If we look at their lives only at the beginning of their sin, it seems like they're having all the fun, and suffering no consequences. Sin is sweet... for a season.

But here's the thing about yeast: after a short while of making bread enticing, it becomes the agent that causes bread to ROT! You know this about bread if you've ever forgotten a sandwich in your backpack for a month. After a while, leavened bread becomes a disgusting, disintegrating lump of filth, fit only for the garbage can. And sin, when it is done puffing up and putting on a beautiful show, will rot away your soul. It will leave you feeling disgusting, like a disintegrating lump of filth, fit only for the garbage can.

There is only one solution for the soul-decaying, body-rotting yeasty sin that can take over your life. And that solution is pointed to in the Feast of Unleavened Bread.

LEAVEN-FREE

The Old Testament predicted that when the Messiah came He would live His entire life without sinning— that He would be entirely "yeast-free." (Read Isaiah 53, it will drop your jaw.) The New Testament tells us that Jesus never sinned (II Corinthians 5:21); that's what made Him the perfect Lamb of God that the Passover required. From His birth until His death He never thought a dirty thought, spoke foolishly, or acted cruelly. Not even once. The Passover required a perfect male Lamb of God, and He was eternally perfect— 100% yeast-free. At His Last Passover dinner, Jesus held up a piece of yeast-free bread and said, "This is My body." Sinless.

The Old Testament also said that the Messiah's body would not rot after it died. "You will not abandon Him to the grave, nor will you let your Holy One see decay (Psalm 16:10)." What an odd clue this is! Scientists tell us that when a person dies, his body begins to decay immediately. But the Bible predicted that the Messiah's body would die, yet it would not decay.

Do you remember my loaf of bread that I made without yeast? For several years I would hold up that little loaf at Bible studies, as an example of what bread was like without yeast. After years in my backpack, it had not rotted. Since it had no yeast, it did not decay. After several years, it looked the same as it did the day I baked it.

Jesus' body, which contained no "leaven," was nailed to the cross, and died at the very hour that Passover lambs all across Jerusalem were being sacrificed. His body was then removed from the cross, and it was placed in a tomb. While His body lay in the grave on that day after Passover, it did not rot. It did not decay. It did not decompose. How do we know? Because on the third day, He walked out of the grave— not as a rotting zombie corpse— but as someone mistaken for the gardener! (But let's not get ahead of ourselves. That's the next chapter.)

Think about it. Jesus' body that had no leaven, lay in the tomb not decaying on *the exact day* of the Feast of Unleavened Bread! The very Feast that looked back to God's not abandoning His people to the graves of Egypt, pointed ahead to God's not abandoning the Messiah's body to the grave. The very Feast that looked back to God's commanding His people to not decay in bondage in Egypt, also pointed ahead to the Messiah who would not decay in the tomb. "You will not abandon Him to the grave, nor will you let your Holy One see decay (Psalm 16:10)." And the Messiah fulfilled all that was prophesied about Him in the Feast of Unleavened Bread *on the very day of* the Feast of Unleavened Bread!

Who, in his wildest imagination,
would have dreamed that the event
to which the Feast had pointed,
year after year, century after century,
would have occurred on the actual day of the Feast?

HOW ABOUT YOU?

HAVE YOU BEEN FREED FROM THE SLAVERY OF SIN THROUGH FAITH IN JESUS? IF YOU PRAYED THE PRAYER AT THE END OF THE LAST CHAPTER, YOU HAVE—IT IS GOD'S PROMISE: "SO IF THE SON SETS YOU FREE, YOU WILL BE FREE INDEED (JOHN 8:36)."

AND IF YOU HAVE BEEN FREED, DO YOU ACT AS IF YOU ARE STILL A SLAVE TO SIN? "DO YOU NOT KNOW THAT IF YOU PRESENT YOURSELVES TO ANYONE AS OBEDIENT SLAVES, YOU ARE SLAVES OF THE ONE YOU OBEY, EITHER OF SIN, WHICH LEADS TO DEATH, OR OF OBEDIENCE, WHICH LEADS TO RIGHTEOUSNESS (ROMANS 6:16)?" IF BY FAITH YOU HAVE RECEIVED THE FREEDOM THAT WAS PURCHASED FOR YOU BY JESUS, THE SPOTLESS, ETERNAL LAMB OF GOD, THEN RUN AWAY FROM YOUR SIN. YOU ARE NOT A SLAVE ANYMORE, SO DON'T ACT LIKE ONE. FLEE YOUR SIN QUICKLY, AND DON'T HARBOR ANY THOUGHT OF REMAINING A CAPTIVE. JUST AS GOD PROVIDED EVERYTHING THAT WAS NECESSARY TO PURCHASE YOUR FREEDOM, HE WILL PROVIDE THE MEANS FOR YOU TO WALK QUICKLY AWAY FROM YOUR "EGYPT." DON'T GIVE THE YEAST A CHANCE TO RISE!

THE THIRD FEAST: FIRSTFRUITS

"But Christ has indeed been raised from the dead, the firstfruits of those
who have fallen asleep
(I Corinthians 15:20)."

O n the day of Passover, God showed His mercy to the children of

Israel, by passing over them in judgment because of the blood of the
lamb. On the next day, He communicated His compassion by
commanding them to leave their slaveholders immediately. They obeyed
Him, and left in such haste that their bread did not even have time to
rise. Now, their flight was underway. We learn the exciting details of
their escape in chapter 14 of the book of Exodus.

Exodus 14

Then the Lord said to Moses, "Tell the people of Israel to
turn back and encamp in front of Pi-hahiroth, between Migdol
and the sea, in front of Baal-zephon; you shall encamp facing it,
by the sea. For Pharaoh will say of the people of Israel, 'They are
wandering in the land; the wilderness has shut them in.' And I
will harden Pharaoh's heart, and he will pursue them, and I will
get glory over Pharaoh and all his host, and the Egyptians shall
know that I am the Lord." And they did so.

When the king of Egypt was told that the people had fled,
the mind of Pharaoh and his servants was changed toward the
people, and they said, "What is this we have done, that we have
let Israel go from serving us?" So he made ready his chariot and

took his army with him, and took six hundred chosen chariots and all the other chariots of Egypt with officers over all of them. And the Lord hardened the heart of Pharaoh king of Egypt, and he pursued the people of Israel while the people of Israel were going out defiantly. The Egyptians pursued them, all Pharaoh's horses and chariots and his horsemen and his army, and overtook them encamped at the sea, by Pi-hahiroth, in front of Baal-zephon. When Pharaoh drew near, the people of Israel lifted up their eyes, and behold, the Egyptians were marching after them, and they feared greatly. And the people of Israel cried out to the Lord. They said to Moses, "Is it because there are no graves in Egypt that you have taken us away to die in the wilderness? What have you done to us in bringing us out of Egypt? Is not this what we said to you in Egypt: 'Leave us alone that we may serve the Egyptians'? For it would have been better for us to serve the Egyptians than to die in the wilderness." And Moses said to the people, "Fear not, stand firm, and see the salvation of the Lord, which He will work for you today. For the Egyptians whom you see today, you shall never see again. The Lord will fight for you, and you have only to be silent."

The Lord said to Moses, "Why do you cry to Me? Tell the people of Israel to go forward. Lift up your staff, and stretch out your hand over the sea and divide it, that the people of Israel may go through the sea on dry ground.

And I will harden the hearts of the Egyptians so that they shall go in after them, and I will get glory over Pharaoh and all his host, his chariots, and his horsemen. And the Egyptians shall know that I am the Lord, when I have gotten glory over Pharaoh, his chariots, and his horsemen."

Then the angel of God who was going before the host of Israel moved and went behind them, and the pillar of cloud moved from before them and stood behind them, coming between the host of Egypt and the host of Israel. And there was the cloud and the darkness. And it lit up the night without one coming near the other all night.

Then Moses stretched out his hand over the sea, and the Lord drove the sea back by a strong east wind all night and made the sea dry land, and the waters were divided. And the people of

Israel went into the midst of the sea on dry ground, the waters being a wall to them on their right hand and on their left. The Egyptians pursued and went in after them into the midst of the sea, all Pharaoh's horses, his chariots, and his horsemen.

And in the morning watch the Lord in the pillar of fire and of cloud looked down on the Egyptian forces and threw the Egyptian forces into a panic, clogging their chariot wheels so that they drove heavily. And the Egyptians said, "Let us flee from before Israel, for the Lord fights for them against the Egyptians."

Then the Lord said to Moses, "Stretch out your hand over the sea, that the water may come back upon the Egyptians, upon their chariots, and upon their horsemen." So Moses stretched out his hand over the sea, and the sea returned to its normal course when the morning appeared. And as the Egyptians fled into it, the Lord threw the Egyptians into the midst of the sea. The waters returned and covered the chariots and the horsemen; of all the host of Pharaoh that had followed them into the sea, not one of them remained. But the people of Israel walked on dry ground through the sea, the waters being a wall to them on their right hand and on their left. Thus the Lord saved Israel that day from the hand of the Egyptians, and Israel saw the Egyptians dead on the seashore. Israel saw the great power that the Lord used against the Egyptians, so the people feared the Lord, and they believed in the Lord and in His servant Moses.

GOD SAVES HIS CHILDREN THROUGH THE WATER

God led His children out of Egypt, by way of the desert wilderness near the Red Sea. During the daytime, in the scorching heat of the desert, He cared for them through His presence in an enormous pillar of cloud that provided shade, and kept them from burning to death. In the evening when the desert turned icy cold and pitch black, He went before them in a pillar of fire, so that they would not freeze to death, nor be frightened in the dark. The first stop they made on their way out of Egypt was to retrieve Joseph's mummy (Exodus 3:19). His coffin had stood in their midst for 400 years, as a constant reminder that God would not abandon them forever to the graves of Egypt. Joseph's bones were going with the children of Israel back to the Promised Land!

But just as God had warned, when Pharaoh learned that the children of Israel were leaving Egypt, he turned against them. He ordered his army, including six hundred choice chariots with captains over each one, to pursue the fleeing free men, and to make them slaves once again. The mightiest army in the world, possessing the finest weaponry of the day, was in hostile pursuit of a band of beaten-down, half-starved, former-slaves, most of whom were women, children and old folks.

Then God did what seems to us a strange thing: He led His children— probably over a million of them, according to scholars— into a dead end! He told them to camp in a place that was walled in on both sides with high cliffs, with the Red Sea in front of them. When they looked behind them, they could see Pharaoh's vast army advancing on them. They were penned in! The only place the people had to flee was into the deep water in front of them. They looked out into Red Sea, and believed they were staring into their graves. The Bible tells us they were "very afraid."

They were so fearful, they regretted having walked in the freedom the Lord had provided for them. They asked Moses why he hadn't let Egypt be their grave (Exodus 14:11). They told him they wished they were still wasting away as slaves.

But God hadn't freed them only to abandon them to the grave. And God hadn't freed them only to send them back to rot in slavery again. And He hadn't freed them to live in paralyzing fear. He freed them to show them His glory. Moses told the people, "Fear not, stand firm, and see the salvation of the Lord, which He will work for you today (Exodus 14:13a)." God led them into a place where only a miracle could save them, so He could save them by a miracle.

And here's how He did it: First, God moved in the pillar that had been in front of His people, to a place behind them, so that He came between His people and their enemy. On the Egyptian side of the pillar, it was a dark cloud— so dark that the Egyptians could not see their target, and they were thrown into confusion. On the Israelites' side of the pillar, it was fire— fire that kept them warm at night, and gave them light to see the next miracle that God was about to do.

Moses then stretched out his hand over the water that lay in front of them, and the Lord caused a strong wind to push the sea back, so that what had looked like a grave to the Israelites was now dry land, with a wall of water on either side. The Israelites crossed over, out of the land of death and slavery, into a new land. They passed through what should have been their grave, and came out on the other side, very much alive.

Pharaoh's army pursued the children of Israel, to try to make them captives once again. They drove their chariots into the bed of the Red Sea— and it became their grave. The walls of water that God had held back for His children came crashing in on their enemies. Throughout all of the surrounding lands for centuries, the people would talk about how mighty the God of Israel was, and how He had fought for His people. As the Hebrew women stood on the banks of the Red Sea, as free women who would soon have more express, God-given rights than any other females in the Ancient World, they gave God the glory and danced and sang, "Sing to the Lord, for He has triumphed gloriously; the horse and his rider He has thrown into the sea (Exodus 15:21)."

The children of Israel were not yet in the land that God had promised to Abraham. They were in the wilderness, and would be for some time. But God promised to take care of them in the desert, and to continue to be the pillar of cloud and of fire that they needed to survive. He told them that when they did arrive in the Promised Land, every year on the day after the Feast of Unleavened Bread, they should hold another Feast, called the Feast of Firstfruits.

FIRSTFRUITS THROUGHOUT ISRAEL'S HISTORY

This Feast of Firstfruits would fall every year *exactly on the anniversary* of the Israelites' rescue by God through the waters of the Red Sea. In God's amazing plan, it was also the exact anniversary of two other very significant events in the history of His people. And they are both related to the Red Sea adventure.

First of all, the date of Firstfruits falls on the same ancient calendar date when Noah and his family landed on dry ground after the worldwide flood (Genesis 8:4).[1] We read in Genesis 6-8 that God was so angry with mankind because of their wickedness and violence that He regretted He had ever made them. He decided that He would judge the earth by covering everyone in it with water. But because of His compassion, He chose to provide the means for Noah's family to be saved through the water. He gave Noah the precise plans for a boat— called an ark— that would survive the tempest He would send. God

Himself closed the door of the ark to preserve them through the water. After about a year on the boat, Noah and his family landed safely on dry ground, saved through the waters of judgment, just as the Israelites were saved through the waters of the Red Sea. Isn't it remarkable that the two times God in His mercy provided a means for His people to be saved through the waters of judgment both share the same anniversary?

That might have been more than enough, like a miraculous blinking sign, to point back to God's miraculous rescues. But, there's *yet another momentous event*— relating to burial and somehow emerging alive through it— that happened, once again, on *the exact date* of the Feast of Firstfruits.

Later on I'm going to tell you about why it took the children of Israel forty years to go fifty miles. Long story short, because of their disobedience, one million Hebrews found themselves stuck for decades in the desert with absolutely no means of feeding themselves. Because of His great mercy, every morning and every evening God sent His children bread that fell from the heavens. It was called "manna," a Hebrew word that means, "What is it?" Every morning and every evening the Israelites received bread from heaven for forty years, until the entire generation of adults that had been freed from slavery had perished in the desert.

Finally, a whole new generation reached the Promised Land— a generation that had only ever tasted bread that came from heaven. And when this new generation had entered the Promised Land, the Bible tells us in Joshua 5:10-12 that the manna stopped falling, and there, for the first time, the people ate food that had sprung from the ground. They enjoyed their first fruits from the earth. Isn't it remarkable that the day upon which the children of Israel ate their first fruits from the Promised Land's earth was the day God had told them to celebrate the Feast of Firstfruits?

CELEBRATING FIRSTFRUITS

To celebrate the Feast, those who were waiting for the Messiah were instructed to set aside annually the very first portion of the very first crop of the year, and present it to the Lord. Every winter, the Hebrew farmers would save a portion of their dry barley seeds and bury them in the ground. Three months later, in the early spring, living shoots would sprout out of the earth. These first sprouts belonged to their

Creator. The priests would mark those first shoots, cut them down, and present them to the Lord. Offering the first part of the harvest to God showed that the farmer had faith in God; He trusted that this would be just the first fruits from the dead earth, and that there would be more to follow.

Every year, those who waited for Messiah would celebrate the Passover. Then on the next day, they would celebrate the Feast of Unleavened Bread. Then, on the third day, they would celebrate the Feast of Firstfruits. When they kept the Feast of Firstfruits, they would think of Noah, who was brought from the land that was judged, who was saved through the waters of the Flood, and who emerged alive to enter a new land. They would think of their ancestors, who were brought from the judged land of Egypt, who were saved through the water of the Red Sea, and who emerged alive to enter a new land. They would think of the generation that was brought out from among those who were judged in the desert, who were saved with manna, and who emerged alive to enter the Promised Land. And they would think about those dead seeds that were brought out, that were buried in the earth, and that emerged alive from the land after three months.

**But God didn't institute the Feast
just to remind His people of what He did;
He wanted to let His children know what He was going to do.**

DESTROY THIS TEMPLE

Again it is Jesus who gives us clues about how the Feast pointed to Himself. Early in Jesus' ministry, He told a group gathered at the Temple, "Destroy this temple, and in three days I will raise it up (John 2:19)." They got very confused about this, because they knew that temples took decades to build. How in the world could Jesus claim to raise up the temple in just three days?

The Bible tells us that Jesus wasn't talking about the Temple in Jerusalem, but He was talking about His own body. Why did Jesus talk this way? Why did He call His body a temple? What was He trying to tell us?

30

SOLOMON'S TEMPLE:
HOME OF THE ARK, CENTER OF WORSHIP, SITE OF THE OFFERINGS

A big part of the answer comes from understanding what exactly the function of the Temple was. During the days of King Solomon and his dynasty in the Kingdom of Judah (which I will tell you about more in Chapter 7), the Temple was the magnificent resting place of the Ark of the Covenant, the focal point of the Israelites' worship, and the site of the sacrificial offerings. The Ark of the Covenant was a gleaming, gold-covered box with statues of golden cherubim-angels atop it. It stood in the architectural center of the Temple, which was located at the geographical center of the Israelites' universe, Jerusalem. It was hidden in the inner sanctum of the Temple, the Holy of Holies, a gold-covered room so sacred it was secluded from the rest of the Temple by golden chains and accessed only by engraved olivewood doors covered in hammered gold. If you touched the Ark of the Covenant, you would die. (I'm not kidding— see for yourself in II Samuel 6.) Only one man, on one day a year was even allowed to look at it. (I'll tell you more about that in Chapter 6.) And why was this magnificent Ark secluded and guarded so? Because the Ark was where the God of Israel, the Ancient of Days, permitted His exquisite glory to reside among men. There, the localized presence of God Almighty dwelt in unapproachable holiness.

Don't get me wrong: God did not reside in the Ark as we live in our houses. No box could hold Him; He fills every space between every atom in the universe. But God did permit some of His radiant, resplendent, stupefying glory to be housed by the Ark.

The Temple was also the center of Hebrew worship. Three times a year, on three of the Feasts— Unleavened Bread, Weeks, and Tabernacles— all the men of Israel were commanded to gather at the Temple. There the Scriptures were read aloud, songs of thanksgiving were sung, and men poured out their hearts in reverent worship. Though men could express adoration to the Lord anywhere and at any time, worshipping in the Temple was unique because of God's intimate, glorious presence there.

Finally, the Temple was where all of Israel's sacrifices occurred. Day in and day out, animals were sacrificed on the altar of the Temple as a covering for the people's sin. The tenth chapter of the New Testament book of Hebrews tells us that these sacrifices themselves had no power to take away sin. They were offered as a covering in anticipation of a greater sacrifice that was coming.2

But what happened to Solomon's magnificent Temple that housed the Ark, was the center of worship, and was the site of the sacrifices? The Babylonians destroyed it in 586 B.C. And what happened to the glorious lost Ark of the Covenant? No one knows. All we do know is that after Solomon's Temple was destroyed, God's glory no longer dwelt on earth. Until...

THE TEMPLE WALKS ON EARTH!

In the fullness of time, God's glory did once again dwell on earth; it dwelt in Jesus Christ! The apostle John talking about Jesus says, "We have seen His glory, glory as of the only Son from the Father, full of grace and truth (John 1:14b)." God's glory once again lived on earth inside Jesus! Just like the Temple was the place where God's glory resided, Jesus' body was the place where God's glory resided. Just as the Temple was the focus of Israel's worship, Jesus is now the focus of our worship. And just as the Temple was the site of all of those sin-covering sacrifices, Jesus body was the place where the ultimate debt-paying sacrifice was inflicted. That's what Jesus meant when He called His body "this temple."

"Destroy this temple, and in three days I will raise it up," Jesus said. And that's just what happened. On the Feast of Passover, Christ our Passover was sacrificed for us. On the Feast of Unleavened Bread, Jesus' sinless body lay in the grave, not decaying. And on the third day, the Feast of Firstfruits, the glory-housing temple named Jesus was raised from the dead. We call that day Easter.

John 20

Now on the first day of the week Mary Magdalene came to the tomb early, while it was still dark, and saw that the stone had been taken away from the tomb. So she ran and went to Simon Peter and the other disciple, the one whom Jesus loved, and said to them, "They have taken the Lord out of the tomb, and we do not know where they have laid Him." So Peter went out with the other disciple, and they were going toward the tomb. Both of them were running together, but the other disciple outran Peter and reached the tomb first. And stooping to look in, he saw the linen cloths lying there, but he did not go in. Then Simon Peter came, following him, and went into the tomb. He saw the linen cloths lying there, and the face cloth, which had been on Jesus' head, not lying with the linen cloths but folded up in a place by itself. Then the other disciple, who had reached the tomb first, also went in, and he saw and believed; for as yet they did not understand the Scripture, that He must rise from the dead. Then the disciples went back to their homes.

But Mary stood weeping outside the tomb, and as she wept she stooped to look into the tomb. And she saw two angels in white, sitting where the body of Jesus had lain, one at the head and one at the feet. They said to her, "Woman, why are you weeping?" She said to them, "They have taken away my Lord, and I do not know where they have laid Him." Having said this, she turned around and saw Jesus standing, but she did not know that it was Jesus. Jesus said to her, "Woman, why are you weeping? Whom are you seeking?" Supposing Him to be the gardener, she said to Him, "Sir, if you have carried Him away, tell me where you have laid Him, and I will take him away." Jesus said to her, "Mary." She turned and said to Him in Aramaic, "Rabboni!" (which means Teacher). Jesus said to her, "Do not cling to me, for I have not yet ascended to the Father; but go to My brothers and say to them, 'I am ascending to My Father and your Father, to My God and your God.'" Mary Magdalene went and announced to the disciples, "I have seen the Lord"— and that He had said these things to her.

On the evening of that day, the first day of the week, the doors being locked where the disciples were for fear of the Jews, Jesus came and stood among them and said to them, "Peace be with you." When He had said this, He showed them His hands and His side. Then the disciples were glad when they saw the Lord. Jesus said to them again, "Peace be with you. As the Father has sent Me, even so I am sending you." And when He had said this, He breathed on them and said to them, "Receive the Holy Spirit. If you forgive the sins of any, they are forgiven them; if you withhold forgiveness from any, it is withheld."

Now Thomas, one of the Twelve, called the Twin, was not with them when Jesus came. So the other disciples told him, "We have seen the Lord." But he said to them, "Unless I see in hands the mark of the nails, and place my finger into the mark of the nails, and place my hand into His side, I will never believe."

Eight days later, His disciples were inside again, and Thomas was with them. Although the doors were locked, Jesus came and stood among them and said, "Peace be with you." Then He said to Thomas, "Put your finger here, and see My hands; and put out your hand, and place it in My side. Do not disbelieve, but believe." Thomas answered Him, "My Lord and my God!" Jesus said to him, "Have you believed because you have seen Me? Blessed are those who have not seen and yet have believed."

Now Jesus did many other signs in the presence of the disciples, which are not written in this book; but these are written so that you may believe that Jesus is the Christ, the Son of God, and that by believing you may have life in His name.

JESUS, THE FIRSTFRUITS

Jesus' body had been dead, dead, dead. Just like the Hebrew farmers would put their dead seeds into the earth, Jesus' dead body was put into the earth. And just as after three months the farmers would see a living thing spring up from the earth, after three days, Jesus living body came out of the earth.

Dead people had been brought back to life prior to this in the Bible; Jesus had brought His friend Lazarus back from the dead only days before. But, nothing like *this* resurrection had ever happened before: Lazarus and all of the others had come back to life in their same, perishable human bodies, in a temporary reprieve until bodily death would claim them once again. Jesus, on the other hand, was raised back to new life with an immortal, imperishable and indestructible body! He was, and still is today, the first one ever to come back from the dead, never to die again.

JESUS' RESURRECTION BODY

Jesus came back to life with a new, amazing body that was totally connected to His old body, yet unique in many ways. Have you ever thought about how different a sunflower seed that you bury in the earth looks from the sunflower that springs from that seed? The seed and the flower don't look a thing alike, yet you know that they are very much connected. The one comes from the other, and they share the same DNA, yet they have quite different attributes.

That's how Jesus' new body, His resurrection body, was connected to the body His mourners had placed into the earth. The one comes from the other, they share the same DNA, yet they have different attributes. When people saw Jesus' resurrection body, they recognized that it was Jesus, yet they saw Him display many amazing new attributes: Yes, they could see Him, touch Him and feel Him. Yes, He ate food just like all of us. No, He wasn't a ghost. And yet, the resurrected Jesus could mysteriously appear and disappear within a room. He could walk through locked doors. He could move great distances at great speed. And, as Acts 1 records it, He had the ability to fly!

Jesus was the first one to come back from the dead, never to die again, and He was the first one to come to life in a resurrection body. That is why the Bible calls Him, "the firstfruits of those who have fallen asleep (I Corinthians 15:20b)." But the Bible tells us that just as the farmer's Firstfruit offering was only the beginning of the harvest, Jesus was just the *firstborn* from among the dead.

YOUR RESURRECTION BODY

The Bible says that if we die before Jesus returns (I'll tell you more about that later too) and our relatives put our bodies down into the grave, our bodies will not remain there forever. When Jesus returns, our bodies will come out of the grave, just like His did. And those who trust in Him will have bodies just like His resurrection body. In John 3:2b it says, "When He appears we shall be like Him, for we shall see Him as He is." (Can you get excited about the flying?)

Jesus told us that after He died, He was going to come out of the grave alive in three days— AND HE DID! Because of that, we can believe Him when He tells us that our dead bodies will come out of the grave alive. (You must read I Corinthians 15— it tells you all about it.) Just as Noah did not remain in the Ark but came out alive, we will come out of the earth alive. Just as the children of Israel did not perish in the Red Sea, but came out alive, we will come out of the earth alive. Just as the Hebrews did not die of starvation in the wilderness, but came out alive, we will come out of the earth alive. And just as a seed placed in the ground does not die there, but comes out of the earth alive, we will come out of the earth alive.

Jesus is the firstfruits from the dead. He raised up the Temple of His body after three days, as He said He would. And He did it on the day of the Feast of Firstfruits.

**Who, in his wildest imagination,
would have dreamed that the event
to which the Feast had pointed,
year after year, century after century,
would have occurred on the actual day of the Feast?**

HOW ABOUT YOU?

DO YOU EVER FEEL THAT GOD HAS LED YOU INTO A DIFFICULT PLACE? DO YOU FEEL THAT PERHAPS YOU'RE ALONE, AND DON'T HAVE A PLACE TO TURN, AND THAT YOUR ENEMIES ARE CLOSING IN ON YOU? ARE YOU AFRAID? MAYBE GOD HAS BROUGHT YOU TO THIS PLACE TO DO A MIRACLE IN YOUR LIFE! MAYBE HE WILL MIRACULOUSLY CHANGE YOUR CIRCUMSTANCES. MAYBE HE WILL WORK IN THE HEARTS OF PEOPLE AROUND YOU. MAYBE HE WILL CHANGE YOU IN AN AMAZING WAY.

REMEMBER, GOD DIDN'T ABANDON YOU TO THE GRAVE THAT WAS YOUR OLD LIFE (OR MAYBE STILL IS, IF YOU HAVEN'T YET TRUSTED YOUR SOUL TO JESUS). AND HE DIDN'T SAVE YOU TO ALLOW YOU TO WALLOW AS A SLAVE TO SIN. JESUS, OUR PASSOVER LAMB, DIED FOR YOU SO THAT HE CAN SHOW HIS GLORY IN YOUR LIFE. LET HIM DO MIRACLES FOR YOU!

THE FOURTH FEAST: WEEKS

"I will betroth you to Me forever; I will betroth you in righteousness and justice, in love and compassion. I will betroth you in faithfulness, and you will acknowledge the Lord (Hosea 2:20-21)."

GOD GIVES HIS LAW

The children of Israel were now liberated from their Egyptian slaveholders. They had crossed the Red Sea, and were free. For hundreds of years they had been told how to live, what to do, and where to go. Now that they were free, they would have to make choices for themselves. But how could they know what were good choices? What standard did they have for choosing right and wrong? How could they know what would please God?

God didn't let them wonder for long. The next part of their amazing journey is found in the book of Exodus, starting in chapter 19 through the end of the book.

Exodus 19:16-19
On the morning of the third day there was thunder and lightning, with a thick cloud over the mountain, and a very loud trumpet blast. Everyone in the camp trembled. Then Moses led the people out of the camp to meet with God, and they stood at the foot of the mountain. Mount Sinai was covered with smoke, because the LORD descended on it in fire. The smoke billowed up from it like smoke from a furnace, the whole mountain trembled violently, and the sound of the trumpet grew louder and louder. Then Moses spoke and the voice of God answered him.

Exodus 24:4-11

Moses then wrote down everything the LORD had said. He got up early the next morning and built an altar at the foot of the mountain and set up twelve stone pillars representing the twelve tribes of Israel. Then he sent young Israelite men, and they offered burnt offerings and sacrificed young bulls as fellowship offerings to the LORD. Moses took half of the blood and put it in bowls, and the other half he sprinkled on the altar. Then he took the Book of the Covenant and read it to the people. They responded, "We will do everything the LORD has said; we will obey."

Moses then took the blood, sprinkled it on the people and said, "This is the blood of the covenant that the LORD has made with you in accordance with all these words."

Moses and Aaron, Nadab and Abihu, and the seventy elders of Israel went up and saw the God of Israel. Under His feet was something like a pavement made of sapphire, clear as the sky itself. But God did not raise His hand against these leaders of the Israelites; they saw God, and they ate and drank.

LET'S MAKE A DEAL

On this day, God made His Law-covenant with Israel. The blood of the covenant sealed the deal, and there was feast to celebrate the covenant. God then told Moses to return to the mountain to "receive tablets of stone, and the law and the commandments which I have written, that you may teach them (Exodus 24:12)."

God did not make His children wonder what they must do to please Him. He explained it to them very carefully in the laws He gave Moses. Not only did He explain it to them, but He made a deal with them. (Bible scholars call a deal a covenant.) He said, "You yourselves have seen what I did to the Egyptians, and how I bore you on eagles' wings and brought you to Myself. Now therefore, if you will indeed obey My voice and keep My covenant, you shall be My treasured possession among all peoples, for all the earth is Mine; and you shall be to Me a kingdom of priests and a holy nation (Exodus 19:4- 6a)."

God said, in effect, I've shown you how powerful I am, and that you can trust Me to keep promises. (Didn't He promise that after 400 years they would leave Egypt?) And now, here is My law; if you obey it, you shall be a treasure to me. For nearly 3500 years, Jews have identified the day upon which God made His covenant with the children of Israel to be 50 days after the Feast of Firstfruits. The day God made the Law-covenant was literally earth shaking. Thunder. Lightning. Smoke. Clouds. Trumpet blasts. Fire. Earth tremors. It was like your house being on fire during an earthquake in the middle of the most terrifying storm you've ever experienced. When God spoke, the ground trembled, and the mountain smoked because He descended upon it in fire. To make it crystal clear what He required of men, God not only spoke His laws for them, He also gave His children the Ten Commandments written with His own hand in tablets of stone. Have you ever memorized them? (Everyone should.)

I AM THE LORD YOUR GOD; YOU SHALL HAVE NO GODS BEFORE ME.
DO NOT WORSHIP IDOLS.
DO NOT TAKE THE LORD'S NAME IN VAIN.
KEEP THE SABBATH HOLY.
HONOR YOUR FATHER AND MOTHER.
DO NOT MURDER.
DO NOT COMMIT ADULTERY.
DO NOT STEAL.
DO NOT BEAR FALSE WITNESS.
DO NOT COVET.

BREAKING THE DEAL

God offered a great deal, the people accepted it, end of story, right? Wrong. After the people agreed to the deal, Moses returned to the mountain, Mount Sinai, to learn more from God (Exodus 24). While Moses was out of sight on the mountain, the Bible says, "The appearance of the glory of the Lord was like a devouring fire on the top of the mountain in the sight of the people of Israel (Exodus 24:17)." The people could continue to see the glory of the Lord on the mountaintop, yet despite the flaming evidence of God's power, they began to question the deal they had made. Was God really there? Would Moses ever come back? Should they make a deal with a different god?

Then the children of Israel did an unthinkable thing: they broke their Law-covenant with God (Exodus 32)! Aaron, Moses' older brother who was supposed to have cared for the people in Moses' absence, told them to gather all their gold jewelry. (Do you remember how the Egyptians had given them gold as they departed on Passover?) He melted down the jewelry, and used an engraving tool to form a statue of a baby cow. Then, gazing at the baby cow statue, the people shouted, "These are your gods, O Israel, who brought you up out of the land of Egypt!"

Can you believe it? They gave their cow figurine the credit for the miracles of Passover and the Red Sea! They broke the first and the second commandments just days after they agreed in the covenant to keep them! Then, they began to behave in a despicably immoral fashion, and caused such a ruckus that Moses' helper Joshua, who was up on the mountain with Moses, thought that the people had been attacked.

God told Moses that, no, there was no attack. That noise was the sound of the people breaking their covenant with Him. Moses came down from the mountain, and was so appalled by what he saw that he threw down and smashed the tablets upon which God had engraved the Ten Commandments. He asked his brother Aaron what the people had done to him that he had brought such a great sin on them. Aaron, formulating the lamest lie a liar ever lied, said that the people gave him their gold, he threw it in the fire, "and out came this calf!" Oh brother.

CONSEQUENCES FOR BREAKING THE DEAL

Moses was ANGRY. And so was God. God told Moses to gather the men who were on His side. Men from Moses' tribe, Levi, responded to this call and stood with Moses. God then instructed Moses to have the Levites go throughout the camp with swords and kill the people who had violated the covenant. Three thousand people were put to death that day! (Do you think God takes covenant-deals seriously?)

> **REMEMBER THIS CLUE AS YOU READ ON:** WHEN ISRAEL MADE ITS COVENANT WITH GOD, THE NATION WAS GATHERED AT THE MOUNT, THE LORD DESCENDED IN FIRE, GOD WROTE HIS LAWS ON TABLETS OF STONE, THE PEOPLE BEHELD THE BLOOD OF THE COVENANT, AND THREE THOUSAND WHO BROKE THE COVENANT PERISHED.

Moses then returned to the mountain for another forty days, where God gave him the Ten Commandments— again (Exodus 34)!

Despite His people's disobedience, God still wanted to be in a covenant relationship with them. He still loved them, and wanted to be their God even though they had turned their backs on Him so quickly. God is slow to anger, and abounding in mercy.

CELEBRATING THE DEAL: THE FEAST OF WEEKS

The Feast of Weeks is the anniversary of the day God made His oath to His people in connection with the Law-covenant. (The Feast is also called "Shavuot" in the Old Testament; that's the Hebrew word for "weeks," and also the Hebrew word for "oath.") The children of Israel were instructed to count off seven weeks and a day (that adds up to fifty days) from the Feast of Firstfruits, then to gather on that late spring day. Attendance was mandatory for all of the men (Exodus 23:17). As they were gathered, they were commanded to present before the Lord two loaves of bread— yeast bread this time. It's a funny way to mark an anniversary, and I'm sure the children of Israel wondered throughout the centuries, "Why does God want us to remember our covenant with Him by presenting two yeast loaves?" I bet the kids wished the loaves were anniversary cake instead!

Year in and year out, the children of Israel would count off seven weeks and a day from the Feast of Firstfruits, then gather together and remember the oath God made with them in the wilderness on Shavuot. Remembering God's oath (*shavuot*) was a great source of joy for them, for they knew that they were the only nation on earth with whom God had made a covenant.

A BITTERSWEET FEAST

But the more they commemorated their covenant with God, the more they realized they had a problem. A big problem. The problem wasn't with the covenant itself; it was a good deal. And the problem wasn't with the One who initiated the covenant; God was faithful and could be trusted to keep His end of the bargain. The problem, the children of Israel knew, was with them. They knew that they hadn't kept the covenant: they had stolen, they had not honored the Sabbath, they had coveted. They were as bad as we are!

Their covenant with God was renewed and was spelled out thoroughly near the end of the books that Moses wrote down in the Bible. (Jews today call those first five books of the Bible the

"Pentateuch," the "Books of the Law," the "Books of Moses" or "The Torah.") In no uncertain terms, the complete covenant said, "Obey the Law, and God will bless you; disobey the Law, and God will punish you (Deuteronomy 28)." The punishment was spelled out and included things like being attacked by their enemies and being made into slaves in a foreign land. Ouch.

In their long history, the Jews would see ample evidence to convince them that God meant what He said in the covenant. In 722 B.C., the Assyrians killed, deported, or enslaved ten of the tribes that had descended from Jacob's twelve sons. They either died, or intermarried, or were taken away to an uncertain fate in Assyria, and they never returned to the Promised Land. People now refer to them as the "Lost Tribes of Israel."

In 586 B.C., the Babylonians took the remaining tribes captive. The descendants of those tribes are the people whom today we call the "Jews." That name comes from the biggest of the tribes that the Babylonians took captive: Judah. (Do you remember which tribe God promised the Messiah would come from? I'll give you a hint: it starts with a "J.")

A NEW DEAL IS PREDICTED

During the Jews' seventy-year captivity in Babylon, God sent them a number of prophets to encourage them. The word "prophet" means "speaks for God," and that's just what the prophets did: they spoke for God. When God had a message for His children, He would tell it to a holy man who would write it down, or say it out loud for God's people.[3]

You have probably heard of some of the prophets God sent to the Jews during their captivity in Babylon. One of them was Daniel, of the lions' den fame. Another was Isaiah, who wrote some of the most stunningly precise predictions about the Messiah in all of the Scriptures. Two others were Jeremiah and Joel, who gave the Jews some very good news. Speaking for God, they told the Jews not to despair over their breaking of the Law-covenant with God. (Theologians call that covenant the "Mosaic Covenant.") Jeremiah and Joel both told the Jews that God had promised that a NEW COVENANT was coming! (Theologians call this covenant the "New Covenant." That's easy to remember.)

Jeremiah 31:31-34

"The time is coming," declares the LORD, "when I will make a new covenant with the house of Israel and with the house of Judah. It will not be like the covenant I made with their forefathers when I took them by the hand to lead them out of Egypt, because they broke My covenant, though I was a husband to them," declares the LORD. "This is the covenant I will make with the house of Israel after that time," declares the LORD. "I will put My law in their minds and write it on their hearts. I will be their God, and they will be My people. No longer will a man teach his neighbor, or a man his brother, saying, 'Know the LORD,' because they will all know Me, from the least of them to the greatest," declares the LORD. "For I will forgive their wickedness and will remember their sins no more."

God said through the prophet Jeremiah, I'm going to make a new covenant with My people, even though they broke our first covenant that I took as seriously as a marriage vow— and we know from the Ten Commandments that God takes marriage vows *very* seriously. (That's what the seventh commandment, "Do not commit adultery," is about.) In this new covenant God promised to write His law on people's hearts, to forgive their wickedness, and to remember their sins no more. The new covenant was not going to depend on His people's obedience; God was going to do all the work. What a message of hope the prophets Jeremiah and Joel brought!

For 1500 years the Feast of Weeks was a bittersweet holiday. On it, the children of Israel would joyfully remember that they were the only nation on earth with whom God had made a covenant. That was truly a unique honor, and it set them apart from every other nation on earth. But on the Feast day, they would also mourn because they had broken that very covenant. Year in and year out, as the people celebrated the Feast of Weeks, they would remember their merciful God, and the amazing covenant He had made with them in the wilderness.

But God didn't institute the Feast
just to remind His people of what He did;
He wanted to let His children know what He was going to do.

Do you remember what Jesus said at His last Passover when He held up the Cup of Redemption? He said, "This is the NEW COVENANT in My blood (I Corinthians 11:25)." The old covenant was ending; the new covenant was *finally* about to begin unfolding! Just as the people in the wilderness beheld the blood of the Mosaic covenant as Moses threw it against the altar and on them, Jesus' friends beheld the blood of the New Covenant that night in the Cup of Redemption.

Jesus was sacrificed on the Feast of Passover, He lay in the grave on the Feast of Unleavened Bread, and He was raised from the dead on the Feast of Firstfruits. The Feast of Weeks was next on the calendar, and just as it had been the anniversary of the Old Covenant, it was going to be the birthday of the New Covenant! Let me explain:

After Jesus' resurrection, He appeared in the vicinity of Jerusalem many times for the next forty days. Sometimes He would meet with only one person at a time; other times He met with groups. Once, He appeared to a gathering of more than five hundred people. The very last time He appeared is recorded in the book of Acts, chapter one. While He was eating with His friends, He told them, "Do not leave Jerusalem, but wait for the gift My Father promised, which you have heard Me speak about. For John baptized with water, but in a few days you will be baptized with the Holy Spirit (Acts 1:4b-5)." Then, He ascended right up into the sky!

His followers did as He instructed. They stayed in Jerusalem, and fifty days after Jesus' resurrection, on the day of the Feast of Weeks, something amazing happened. Since the New Testament was written in Greek and not Hebrew, it uses the Greek word for fifty when it refers to the Feast of Weeks: Pentecost.

Acts 2:1-41

When the day of Pentecost came, they were all together in one place. Suddenly a sound like the blowing of a violent wind came from heaven and filled the whole house where they were sitting. They saw what seemed to be tongues of fire that separated and came to rest on each of them. All of them were filled with the Holy Spirit and began to speak in other tongues as the Spirit enabled them.

Now there were staying in Jerusalem God-fearing Jews from every nation under heaven. When they heard this sound, a crowd came together in bewilderment, because each one heard them speaking in his own language. Utterly amazed, they asked: "Are not all these men who are speaking Galileans? Then how is it that each of us hears them in his own native language? Parthians, Medes and Elamites; residents of Mesopotamia, Judea and Cappadocia, Pontus and Asia, Phrygia and Pamphylia, Egypt and the parts of Libya near Cyrene; visitors from Rome (both Jews and converts to Judaism); Cretans and Arabs- we hear them declaring the wonders of God in our own tongues!" Amazed and perplexed, they asked one another, "What does this mean?"

Some, however, made fun of them and said, "They have had too much wine."

Then Peter stood up with the Eleven, raised his voice and addressed the crowd: "Fellow Jews and all of you who live in Jerusalem, let me explain this to you; listen carefully to what I say. These men are not drunk, as you suppose. It's only nine in the morning! No, this is what was spoken by the prophet Joel: 'In the last days, God says, I will pour out My Spirit on all people. Your sons and daughters will prophesy, your young men will see visions your old men will dream dreams. Even on My servants, both men and women, I will pour out My Spirit in those days, and they will prophesy. I will show wonders in the heaven above and signs on the earth below, blood and fire and billows of smoke. The sun will be turned to darkness and the moon to blood before the coming of the great and glorious day of the Lord. And everyone who calls on the name of the Lord will be saved.'

"Men of Israel, listen to this: Jesus of Nazareth was a man accredited by God to you by miracles, wonders and signs, which God did among you through Him, as you yourselves know. This man was handed over to you by God's set purpose and foreknowledge; and you, with the help of wicked men, put Him to

death by nailing Him to the cross. But God raised Him from the dead, freeing Him from the agony of death, because it was impossible for death to keep its hold on Him. David said about Him: 'I saw the Lord always before me. Because He is at my right hand, I will not be shaken. Therefore my heart is glad and my tongue rejoices; my body also will live in hope, because You will not abandon me to the grave, nor will you let Your Holy One see decay. You have made known to me the paths of life; You will fill me with joy in Your presence.'

"Brothers, I can tell you confidently that the patriarch David died and was buried, and his tomb is here to this day. But he was a prophet and knew that God had promised him on oath that He would place one of his descendants on his throne. Seeing what was ahead, he spoke of the resurrection of the Christ, that He was not abandoned to the grave, nor did His body see decay. God has raised this Jesus to life, and we are all witnesses of the fact. Exalted to the right hand of God, He has received from the Father the promised Holy Spirit and has poured out what you now see and hear. For David did not ascend to heaven, and yet he said, 'The Lord said to my Lord: "Sit at My right hand until I make Your enemies a footstool for Your feet.'"

"Therefore let all Israel be assured of this: God has made this Jesus, whom you crucified, both Lord and Christ." When the people heard this, they were cut to the heart and said to Peter and the other apostles, "Brothers, what shall we do?" Peter replied, "Repent and be baptized, every one of you, in the name of Jesus Christ for the forgiveness of your sins. And you will receive the gift of the Holy Spirit. The promise is for you and your children and for all who are far off—for all whom the Lord our God will call." With many other words he warned them; and he pleaded with them, "Save yourselves from this corrupt generation." Those who accepted his message were baptized, and about three thousand were added to their number that day.

THE NEW DEAL REPLACES THE OLD DEAL

On that Pentecost— that first Feast of Weeks after Jesus' resurrection— God inaugurated, or started up, the New Covenant. *And He did it on the anniversary of the inauguration of the Old Covenant!*

All the men who were parties to the Old Covenant were gathered in Jerusalem, on Mount Zion, as they were commanded to do on the Feast of Weeks. While they were there on the Mount, God descended in fire. When Peter spoke and explained to them that this was the start of the New Covenant that the prophet Joel had predicted, three thousand believed and were baptized. (Baptism, called a "mikveh" in Hebrew, was a ritual in the Old Testament that signified a person was entering into a covenant. It was a ceremonial bath a person took to demonstrate that he was forsaking— washing away— his old allegiances and forming a new covenant.)

IS IT A COINCIDENCE?

Isn't it interesting that on the day the Old Covenant was inaugurated, fifty days after God had freed His people from slavery, the covenant people were gathered on Mount Sinai, God descended in fire, He wrote His law in stone, and three thousand people who broke the covenant perished. On the day the New Covenant was inaugurated, fifty days after God had freed His people from slavery to sin, the covenant people were gathered at Mount Zion, God descended in fire, He wrote His law in their hearts, and three thousand people entered into the covenant and were baptized! And both events— the inaugurations of both the Old Covenant and the New Covenant— happened on the Feast of Weeks, AKA: Pentecost!

TWO LOAVES

Do you remember the two loaves of bread that were presented before the Lord, year in and year out on the Feast of Weeks? For centuries, I'm sure the Jews wondered, what was God pointing to with those two loaves? On Pentecost, the mystery was revealed. The third chapter of the New Testament book of Ephesians tells us that there had been a plan, "not made known to the sons of men in other generations," but now revealed: the Gentiles get to be a part of the New Covenant too! (A Gentile is anyone who is not an Israelite.) Both Jew and Gentile are "fellow heirs" of the covenant, and those heirs are called collectively "the church."

When you hear the word "church," you might think of a tall building with stain glass windows and a steeple pointing to the sky. That's a church *building*. But "the church" is the name for all the people in the world who have entered into the New Covenant. And entering into the New Covenant is simple, as Peter explained at Pentecost, "Everyone who calls on the name of the Lord shall be saved (Acts 2:21b)." If you call on the Lord, you get to enter the New Covenant. You don't have to promise to keep the law to enter the Covenant; you just have to call on His name.

The two loaves of bread on the Feast of Weeks pointed to the fact that there would be two groups of people who were parties to the New Covenant. One group would be descendants of those who were a party to the Old Covenant (the Jews), and other group would be descendants of people who had never ever had a covenant with God before (the Gentiles). Call one group the Jewish loaf, and the other the Gentile loaf. At Pentecost, the time had come when the two loaves came together to make an amazing new sandwich called "the church."

Not all of the promises included in the New Covenant and vowed to the church were fulfilled at Pentecost. There are some aspects of the New Covenant that will unfold in the future. You'll learn more about those if you keep reading this book.

THE FEAST OF WEEKS: A LOVE STORY

Interestingly, for thousands of years, and still to this day, when Jewish people gather to celebrate the Feast of Weeks, they read aloud the Old Testament book of Ruth. This book does not take place during the Exodus time of wandering in the wilderness, rather, it is set around four hundred years later. It is a beautiful love story of a Gentile woman and a Jewish man who come together to make a covenant of marriage. Their great-grandson, we learn, is King David (from the David and Goliath story) of the tribe of Judah. Later, God tells King David that the Messiah will be one of his descendants. (I'll tell you more about King David in Chapter 6.)

Isn't it fascinating that every year on the Feast when the Jews celebrate their covenant with God, they continue to read a story about a covenant between a Jew and a Gentile? The story of a covenant, the fruit of which is the promised Messiah? For all those centuries, they had no way of knowing that the promised New Covenant would bring Jews and Gentiles together through the Messiah on the Feast of Weeks. Yet on the Feast of Weeks every year, they read the story of a Jew and Gentile coming together in a covenant that produced the Messiah.

Another interesting custom that some Jews practice when they are gathered in synagogues on the Feast of Weeks, is to re-enact a marriage ceremony, under a wedding canopy called a "chupah." They believe that when God made His covenant with His people, it was like a marriage between them, and so they conduct a "wedding" to remember their vows. During the ceremony at the synagogue, a marriage covenant called a "ketubah" is read, and the sacred Jewish book *The Talmud* calls this day, "The Marriage Day between God and His people, between heaven and earth." Some ketubahs contain beautiful quotes from the Old Testament, like: "I will betroth thee unto Me forever; I will betroth thee unto Me in righteousness, and in justice, and in loving kindness, and in compassion. And I will betroth thee unto Me in faithfulness, and thou shalt know the Lord (Hosea 2:19-20)."

Do you remember that in the description of the New Covenant in Jeremiah 31:32, God Himself said that His covenant was like a marriage covenant? He said, "I was a husband to them." A marriage covenant was, and still is the most sacred promise a person could ever make. When two parties enter into a marriage covenant, they solemnly swear that they will be faithful to each other and belong to each other forever. God wanted us to think about the New Covenant this way because, in the last book of the Bible, the name He gave to the Church, His partner in the covenant, was "the Bride of Christ."

BETROTHALS AND WEDDINGS IN BIBLE TIMES

We can understand even more about God's covenant with the "Bride of Christ" if we know more about weddings in Jesus' day. Back in Bible times, when a father had a son who was ready to marry, the father would go out and choose a bride for his son. The father would go to the bride's household and pay a very large price for the bride, and give the bride gifts. Then the bride and groom would make a solemn promise that they would be faithful to each other, and seal the promise by drinking the wine of the covenant. This was called their betrothal, and it was a binding, permanent, legal contract. Right after the bride agreed to the betrothal, she would privately take her marital mikveh bath, to show that she was entering into this covenant with the groom.

Then, the groom would leave! The marriage contract was a done deal; the bride and groom were permanently committed to each other. It was not like what we call an "engagement," where two people are merely planning to get married; it was more like the wedding ceremony itself, but without a wedding night. Although the marriage covenant was already in effect, the marriage wasn't consummated, and the bride and groom didn't get to live or sleep together yet.

In fact, upon the betrothal, the groom would go back to his father's house to prepare a place for his new wife, and the bride would stay behind with her family. As the groom left, he would make a promise to return to the bride, something like, "I go to prepare a place for you. If I go and prepare a place for you I will return to receive you to myself, that where I am you may be also."

After a Jewish betrothal during Bible times, the bride didn't know when the groom would return, only that he promised to return when his father said it was time— and only his father knew the time. While the groom was away, the bride would make herself ready for the groom so that when he returned she would be very attractive to him. She didn't want to be found with her hair and face a mess or her clothes dirty. Then, one night, when the groom's father said it was time, the groom, along with some of his friends, would make the trip to the bride's house. Ever so quietly, he would approach her house, delighting to surprise her with his arrival. Just as he came to her house, one of his groomsmen would let out a shout and blow a trumpet. Then the groom would scoop up his wife, covered in a veil and soon enrobed in a beautiful gown that his father had provided for her, and take her away to the home he had prepared for her.

The two newlyweds would stay secluded in the bridal chamber, enjoying each other for seven full days. This was kind of like what we call a "honeymoon," only the bride and groom weren't away on a trip; they were at their home. When the seven days were over, the groom would lead his wife out and lift off her veil to show everyone his beautiful bride.

Then there would be a great wedding feast. This was kind of like what we call a "wedding reception dinner," with eating and drinking and dancing and singing— a joyous celebration.

CHRIST'S BETROTHAL TO HIS BRIDE

The Feast of Pentecost was the time of the Church's covenant betrothal to Christ. On that day, the bride the Father had chosen for

Christ made her solemn commitment to Him. The three thousand who believed that day had their mikveh— their baptism. The Father had already paid an enormous price for the bride— the death of His only Son. But that day He also gave the gift Jesus had promised was coming— the Holy Spirit.

But now it was time for the bride to wait. Just a few weeks before, on the Passover, when Jesus drank the wine of the covenant, the groom had made His promise to return. In John 14 He had said, "Behold, I go to prepare a place for you. And if I go and prepare a place for you, I will return to receive you, so that where I am you may be also."

If you have called upon the name of the Lord Jesus Christ, you are a part the New Covenant— you are a part of the Bride of Christ. Right now the Bride of Christ is preparing herself, beautifying herself, and eagerly awaiting the return of the groom, Jesus, to take her (us!) to His Father's house. As we wait, we want to be pure. We don't want our groom to be ashamed of us when He comes. We don't know when He'll come, only that He's promised to come. And fascinating clues about His return are found in the next Feast, so keep reading.

God kept His promise, and replaced the Old Covenant that His children wouldn't keep, with the New Covenant that He kept for them. This New Covenant is His solemn betrothal to anyone who wants to belong to Him. And He delivered the New Covenant on the exact anniversary of the Old Covenant, the Feast of Weeks!

**Who, in his wildest imagination,
would have dreamed that the event
to which the Feast had pointed,
year after year, century after century,
would have occurred on the actual day of the Feast?**

HOW ABOUT YOU?

AFTER MOSES HAD BEEN ON THE MOUNTAIN WITH GOD FOR FORTY DAYS, SOMETHING AMAZING HAPPENED TO MOSES' FACE: IT BEGAN TO GLOW (EXODUS 34:29-35)! HE HAD BEEN FOR SO LONG IN THE DAZZLING, CONSUMING PRESENCE OF ALMIGHTY GOD, THAT HIS FACE RADIATED GOD'S GLORY.

DO YOU KNOW ANY PEOPLE LIKE THAT? BELIEVERS WHO LOVE THE LORD SO MUCH, OBEY HIS LAWS SO JOYFULLY, AND SPEND SUCH HAPPY MOMENTS PRAYING TO HIM, THAT THEY SEEM TO GLOW? (I MEAN THAT IN THE FIGURATIVE SENSE.) THE BIBLE SAYS, "THOSE WHO LOOK TO HIM ARE RADIANT (PSALM 34:5)."

YOU CAN BE ONE OF THOSE PEOPLE. SET ASIDE TIME EACH DAY TO SPEND IN GOD'S PRESENCE PRAYING TO HIM AND STUDYING THE BIBLE. DAY BY DAY, YOUR LIFE WILL CHANGE AS YOU GET TO KNOW HIM BETTER. AND JUST LIKE THE MOON HAS NO LIGHT OF ITS OWN BUT GLEAMS IN THE SKY BECAUSE IT REFLECTS THE LIGHT OF THE SUN, YOU COULD BEGIN TO GLOW AS YOU REFLECT THE LIGHT OF THE SON.

PART TWO:

THE FALL FEASTS

THE FIFTH FEAST: TRUMPETS

"For the trumpet will sound, the dead will be raised imperishable, and
we will be changed
(I Corinthians 15:52b)."

SPRING FEASTS AND FALL FEASTS

God saved the children of Israel from the angel of death on Passover. On the next day, He told them to leave their slaveholders quickly. On the following day, He led them through the Red Sea, as on dry ground. Fifty days later, God gave His children the Law.

Part of God's Law contained the commandment to keep four spring feasts, and three fall feasts. The four spring feasts were to commemorate the events of the Exodus from Egypt that had just transpired. The three fall feasts were given to be a commemoration of the events that were *going* to occur as God established His people in the Promised Land.

STANDING BEFORE THE PROMISED LAND

Do you remember that nearly six hundred years earlier, God had promised Abraham that his descendants would have their own land? God even specified the boundaries. After four hundred years in bondage, the time had finally arrived for the children of Abraham to enter the Promised Land, Canaan. Can you imagine how excited they were?

The land God had prepared for His children was not barren wilderness. It was cultivated land, with wells dug and vineyards planted. The problem was, it was inhabited by people whose practices were abhorrent to God.

All of the people staying in the land God had promised to Abraham worshiped idols. For many of them, their worship included vile practices like placing their babies on a flaming altar to be burnt alive, or offering their little children to be temple prostitutes, or other disgusting acts that are described in the eighteenth chapter of Leviticus, but which I can't list here or your parents wouldn't let you read this book.

God had judged these revolting, detestable practices, and had told His children that they were to be His agents as He drove these idol worshipers from His holy land. "It is on account of the wickedness of these nations that the Lord is going to drive them out before you (Deuteronomy 9:4b)," Moses told them. God would fight the battle for them, just like He had conquered Pharaoh's army for them. "The Lord your God Himself will drive them out of your way. He will push them out before you, and you will take possession of their land as the Lord your God promised you (Joshua 23:5-6)."

To prepare for entering the land, Moses sent out twelve spies (Numbers 13). For forty days, they explored Canaan, and collected some of its fruit. They returned to the camp carrying a cluster of grapes so large they had to hang it on a pole that required two men to carry! They reported, "We came to the land to which you sent us. It flows with milk and honey, and this is its fruit (Numbers 13:27)." The land God had promised was indeed good.

FOCUSING ON GIANTS

But then, the spies began to focus on the enemy, even though God had already told them He would fight the enemy for them. They fearfully reported, "However, the people who dwell in the land are strong, and the cities are fortified and very large. And besides, we saw the descendants of Anak (giants) there...We are not able to go up against the people, for they are stronger than we...It is a land that devours its inhabitants, and all the people we saw in it are of great height (Numbers 13:28, 31b, 32b)."

The people replied:

Numbers 14:2b-4

"Would that we had died in the land of Egypt! Or would that we had died in this wilderness! Why is the Lord bringing us into this land, to fall by the sword? Our wives and our little ones will become a prey. Would it not be better for us to go back to Egypt?" And they said to one another, "Let us choose a leader and go back to Egypt."

The gathered congregation forgot about the milk, honey, and enormous grape clusters. They forgot about God's faithfulness in the past. They ignored God's promise to fight the enemy for them. All they thought about were GIANTS. The more they thought about them, the bigger they grew in their minds.

They complained mightily, wishing that Egypt had been their grave. Or that they had died in the wilderness. Anything but fight giants.

They should have been careful what they wished for. In the Feast of Unleavened Bread, God had already illustrated that He was not going to abandon them to the graves of Egypt. But if dying in the desert was what they wanted, that was what they were going to get:

Numbers 14:21-23

"But truly, as I live, and as all the earth shall be filled with the glory of the Lord, none of the men who have seen My glory and My signs that I did in Egypt and in the wilderness and yet have put Me to the test these ten times, and have not obeyed My voice, shall see the land that I swore to give their fathers. And none of those that despised Me shall see it."

GOD PUNISHES HIS CHILDREN

Only the kids under the age of 20 were going to enter the Promised Land. The generation that had doubted God was going to remain in the wilderness until they had all died, just like they wished. God said that their time in the desert would last one year for each of the days the spies had spent in Canaan— forty years!

During those forty years, God still loved His covenant people. He continued to provide them manna and quail daily. He gave them water daily. He sustained them through the pillar of cloud and fire daily. He even made sure their shoes didn't wear out for forty years! But the generation that doubted God after witnessing His miracles perished in the desert. Only two men from that group, Joshua and Caleb, were permitted to enter Canaan.

FINALLY ENTERING THE PROMISED LAND

Finally, finally, the journey that could have taken three days, but instead lasted forty years, ended. Under the leadership of Joshua, the people crossed the Jordan River (which God dried up for them just as He had the Red Sea), and they entered the Promised Land (Joshua 3). Their first task was to take the city of Jericho.

Joshua 6:1-5,20

Now Jericho was tightly shut up because of the Israelites. No one went out and no one came in. Then the LORD said to Joshua, "See, I have delivered Jericho into your hands, along with its king and its fighting men. March around the city once with all the armed men. Do this for six days. Have seven priests carry trumpets of rams' horns in front of the ark. On the seventh day, march around the city seven times, with the priests blowing the trumpets. When you hear them sound a long blast on the trumpets, have all the people give a loud shout; then the wall of the city will collapse and the people will go up, every man straight in."

When the trumpets sounded, the people shouted, and at the sound of the trumpet, when the people gave a loud shout, the wall collapsed; so every man charged straight in, and they took the city.

As the people took their inheritance in the Promised Land, they blew the trumpet and let out a shout; then God gave them the victory. On the Feast of Trumpets, His children were instructed to blow a ram's horn trumpet called a shofar. Every year when the shofar blew on the Feast of Trumpets, the children of Israel could remember how, many years after God had made His covenant betrothal with His people, by means of a miracle, He brought them to the inheritance He had prepared for them.

And could it be,
that just as God might have delivered the fall Feasts
to point ahead to a time
when the children of Israel would dwell in
the Promised Land,
that those Feasts might still point ahead to a time
when Jesus the Messiah will return to dwell in
the Promised Land?

THE GROOM'S RETURN

Just as God instituted the Feast of Trumpets before the event it invokes occurred, perhaps the Feast of Trumpets now points to something that hasn't yet occurred. Jesus made His covenant betrothal to His bride the church, and then said that He was going away to prepare a place for her. Like a good Jewish groom, He promised that He would return. And now the Bride of Christ waits for the day when Jesus returns for her.

But what are we waiting for? What will it be like when Jesus returns for us? When will that happen? The Bible gives us many of these answers.

Matthew 24:31

And He will send His angels with a great sound of a trumpet, and they will gather together His elect from the four winds, from one end of heaven to the other.

1 Corinthians 15:51-53

Listen, I tell you a mystery: We will not all sleep, but we will all be changed— in a flash, in the twinkling of an eye, at the last trumpet. For the trumpet will sound, the dead will be raised imperishable, and we will be changed. For the perishable must clothe itself with the imperishable, and the mortal with immortality.

1 Thessalonians 4:15-17

According to the Lord's own word, we tell you that we who are still alive, who are left till the coming of the Lord, will certainly not precede those who have fallen asleep. For the Lord Himself will come down from heaven, with a loud command, with the voice of the archangel and with the trumpet call of God, and the dead in Christ will rise first. After that, we who are still alive and are left will be caught up together with them in the clouds to meet the Lord in the air. And so we will be with the Lord forever.

When Jesus returns for His bride there will be a shout and a trumpet call, just like there was at Jericho, and just like there always was when a Jewish groom returned for his bride. Then everyone who is a part of the bride, living or dead, will be swept up from the earth to be with Jesus in the sky. (Remember I told you about flying?) Theologians call this event "the rapture," and it is the glorious hope of everyone who loves the Lord. Jesus will take His bride home to the place He has been preparing for us since He left.

Just as in Joshua's time there was a shout and a trumpet call before the people were brought into the place God had prepared for them, so in the End Times there will be a shout and a trumpet call before Jesus brings us to the place He has prepared for us. For 3500 years, the Feast of Trumpets has harkened to the time when God miraculously delivered His covenant people's promised inheritance, and now perhaps points ahead to when God will provide His covenant bride's promised inheritance.

WHEN WILL THE GROOM RETURN?

For how many more years might the Feast point ahead to what Jesus is going to do? When will He return for His bride as He promised?

Interestingly, the Feast of Trumpets is the only Feast for which we do not have a precise date. It comes on the new moon in the month of Tishri— September or October. The problem with a new moon is that it is so slender, it's hard to detect. Jewish priests used to stand watch to determine when it had arrived. When the witnesses saw the new moon, they would blow their shofar-trumpets. The Feast of Trumpets was, and is, a great day of joy for the Jews, and it ushers in what they call the "Days of Awe," the most holy time of the year.

60

Just as the priests didn't know the precise day of the Feast of Trumpets, we don't know the precise day that the Lord will return. Just as a Jewish groom didn't know the time of his return, but would come when his father sent him, Jesus said that only Father knows the time of His return. But has the Father given us any clues? Perhaps so!

6 AND 1

Here is a theory for you to ruminate: According to Judaism, we are living near the end of the sixth millennium. Cornerstones of orthodox synagogues in the United States are all inscribed with years in the 5600's or 5700's. The Orthodox Jews believe that there have been almost six thousand years since God created Adam. Bishop Usher, the famous historian of the church, came up with a similar estimate, as did Sebastian C. Adams in his perennially classic timeline of human history. If you add together all of the life spans of the generations provided in Genesis, it places us now just a little shy of six thousand years from Adam.

In the Bible, there is a repeated pattern of six and one. Exodus 20:11 tells us, "For in six days the LORD made the heavens and the earth, the sea, and all that is in them, and rested the seventh day." God appointed for man six days for work, but the seventh was the Sabbath for rest— that's from the Ten Commandments. God said that for six years His children could work the land, but in the seventh year, the land must receive a rest.

The Scriptures tell us that the earth has been laboring under the curse of the Fall since the time of Adam— almost six thousand years. It also says that there is a one thousand-year Sabbath rest coming for the people of God. (Jesus refers to it as the Kingdom, and I'm going to tell you more about that in the last chapter of this book.) Could it be possible that we are closing in on the end of the six thousand years of labor, and approaching the beginning of our one thousand years of rest, to be ushered in by trumpets?

DO WE HAVE A CLUE?

And what time of the year do you think it will be when Jesus returns to finally take His bride home, as suggested in the Feast of Trumpets? Since the events depicted in the Feast of Passover occurred *on* the Feast of Passover, and the events depicted in the Feast of

Unleavened Bread occurred *on* the Feast of Unleavened Bread, and the events depicted in the Feast of Firstfruits occurred *on* the Feast of Firstfruits, and the events depicted in the Feast of Weeks occurred *on* the Feast of Weeks, do you think God has given us a hint about when the events suggested in the Feast of Trumpets might occur?

Jesus told His disciples that only the Father knew the time of His coming, but He also rebuked the Pharisees for not interpreting the signs about the future that He had provided in His Word (Matthew 16:2-4). I don't know when Jesus will return for me, but I try to keep myself ready to meet Him, and every fall when I see on the calendar that the Feast of Trumpets is approaching, my heart skips a beat, and I find myself scanning the sky a bit.

HAPPY NEW YEAR

Modern Jews often call the Feast of Trumpets by its nickname, Rosh Hashanah, which means "Head of the Year." They call it this because it is the start of their civil calendar, their "New Year's Day." (Do you remember that I explained in Chapter 3 that Judaism has both a civil and religious calendar?) How interesting it is that Rosh Hashanah— the Feast of Trumpets— might mark the beginning of not just a new year when Jesus comes, but a new Kingdom, our new bodies, a new order to the universe. It will be the newest year that ever there was since the Creation!

More traditional Jews sometimes call the Feast of Trumpets by another nickname: The Wedding Day of the Messiah. The word for wedding in Hebrew means "home-going." And that is exactly what the Lord's trumpets will herald, perhaps one day soon: it will be the day when Jesus returns to take us home.

Perhaps, just perhaps,
the event which the Feast has invoked,
year after year, century after century,
will occur on the actual day of the Feast!

HOW ABOUT YOU?

DO YOU EVER DOUBT THAT GOD HAS YOUR BEST INTEREST AT HEART? DO YOU EVER QUESTION WHAT GOD HAS CHOSEN FOR YOU? THE CHILDREN OF ISRAEL HAD AMPLE EVIDENCE THAT GOD CARED FOR THEM, THAT HE HAD THEIR BEST INTEREST AT HEART, AND THAT HE HAD THE POWER TO DO MIRACLES. YET THEY QUESTIONED HIS PLAN FOR THEM. THEY WISHED FOR SOMETHING THAT WAS MUCH WORSE THAN GOD'S DESIRE FOR THEM.

YOUR CIRCUMSTANCES ARE NOT A SURPRISE TO GOD. THE BOOK OF ROMANS TELLS US, "ALL THINGS WORK TOGETHER FOR GOOD FOR THOSE WHO LOVE THE LORD, WHO ARE CALLED ACCORDING TO HIS PURPOSE (ROMANS 8:28)." IF JESUS IS YOUR SAVIOR, YOU ARE THE APPLE OF HIS EYE. HE HAS A PLAN FOR YOUR LIFE THAT WILL PROSPER YOU FOR ALL ETERNITY. IF YOUR CIRCUMSTANCES SEEM DIFFICULT NOW, IT COULD BE THAT HE IS PREPARING YOU FOR SOMETHING TRULY AMAZING.

DON'T WASTE YOUR TIME WISHING YOU HAD SOMETHING OTHER THAN WHAT GOD HAS APPOINTED FOR YOU. TRUST HIM, AND WAIT TO SEE HIS MARVELOUS PLAN FOR YOUR LIFE.

THE SIXTH FEAST:

THE DAY OF ATONEMENT

"He will be great and be called the Son of the Most High. The Lord God will give Him the throne of His father David, and He will reign over the house of Jacob forever; His kingdom will never end (Luke 1:32-33)."

LIFE IN THE PROMISED LAND

The children of Israel had finally entered the Promised Land, and if they had obeyed as *they* had promised, they would have ruled the land and had rest from their enemies quickly. But they didn't. The Old Testament book of Judges describes the next four hundred years of their time in the Promised Land. It details a cycle that they would repeat over and over again.

First, Israel (as the nation was now called) would break their covenant with God by worshipping idols. Then, an enemy would attack them. In their distress, Israel would repent of their idol worship. In response to their repentance, God would raise up a military leader that the Bible calls a "judge." The judge would lead Israel to victory over its enemy. But after a while, Israel would begin to worship idols again, and the cycle would repeat. Some of the famous judges God raised up to lead His people to victory were Samson (of Samson and Delilah fame), Gideon, and Deborah. The last judge of Israel, Samuel, had a special job to do.

A KINGDOM COMES

Throughout the period of the judges, the people would often complain, "All the other nations have a king; why can't we have a king?" (Have you ever heard children who want something from their parents use similar tactics?) Eventually, God gave them a king, and the last judge, Samuel, was the one to anoint him.

"Anointing" in the Bible was how someone was set apart for a special job like king or priest. God would indicate to one of His prophets the man He had appointed for that special job, and instruct the prophet to take oil and pour it on top of that man's head. You might get angry if someone poured oil on your head, but if a prophet in the Bible did it to you, it meant God had a very special plan for you.

Samuel first anointed king a man named Saul from the tribe of Benjamin. God told Saul that if he were faithful, he could have a dynasty. (A dynasty is when the king's son becomes king, and his son becomes king, and so on.) But Saul wasn't faithful, he had no dynasty, and Samuel had to anoint a new king.

The man Samuel anointed next was from the tribe of Judah, and he was the most famous of all the kings of Israel, King David. When David was a teenager, he slew the nine-foot-tall Goliath, one of the descendants of the giants Joshua's spies were so afraid of. As a young man he was a valiant soldier, leading Israel to victory over tens of thousands of soldiers. When he was thirty years old, he became king of Israel.

DAVID'S SIN

One day during David's reign, before he had completely routed Israel's enemies, he was walking around on the roof of his palace. From that vantage point he could see a woman in her house taking a bath. Instead of looking away, as a proper gentleman would, he kept looking. He then had the woman, named Bathsheba, brought to him. Even though David knew Bathsheba was married to another man, he did things with her that a man must never do with a woman who is not his wife.

As a result of David's illicit encounter with Bathsheba, she became pregnant. When David learned this, he tried to make it look like the father of the baby was Bathsheba's husband. That plan backfired, so David had Bathsheba's husband killed, and then took Bathsheba as his wife.

Can you believe it? The King of Israel, a person the Bible calls, "a man after God's own heart," committed adultery *and* murder! God sent the prophet Nathan to confront David, and to convict him of his sin.

DAVID REPENTS

When you are convicted of sinfulness in your life, you can do one of two things. You can ignore the guilt and conviction you feel, pretending it was no big deal, stuffing it down to fester and rot like a piece of moldy bread in your soul. The Bible says if you do this long enough, your conscience becomes seared so that after a while, you can't even feel remorse for sin anymore.

The other response you can have to the conviction of sin in your life is to admit that you were wrong, confess your sin to God, and throw yourself on His mercy.

That's what David did. He mourned his sin. He poured out his heart in repentance to God. He threw himself upon the mercy of the One enthroned on the Mercy Seat.

Not only did David say these penitent prayers, he also wrote them down and set them to music, in the most beautiful songbook ever written, called the Book of Psalms. If you crack open your Bible to the dead center, you'll be in the Book of Psalms.

There are 150 Psalms (*psalm* is the Hebrew word for song), and David wrote most of them. In this, Israel's hymnal, the king led the nation in repentance and acknowledgement of their utter dependence on God. If you ever want words to use in repentance to God for a sin you've committed, pray Psalm 51 out loud to God. Many holy people in history have borrowed these words of mourning as they've approached the throne of God in prayer.

DAVID SUBDUES HIS ENEMIES

By the end of David's reign, he had subdued all of his enemies in the Promised Land, so that his successor enjoyed a kingdom of peace. Here is a list of some of the idol-worshipping enemies David defeated before he died: Philistines, Moabites, Syrians, Arameans, Edomites, Amorites, Hittites, Jebusites, Amalekites, and Ammonites.

DAVID SITS ON HIS THRONE BEFORE HIS PEOPLE

Finally, the nation of Israel could come before their king, seated on his throne in the Promised Land. In the book of I Chronicles, chapters 28 and 29, David calls before his throne all the representatives of the people— leaders of the tribes, of the military, and of the palace— to remind them of their responsibility before God and to implore them to "Bless the Lord our God (I Chronicles 29:20)."

During his reign, David led the nation in mourning and repentance from sin, he finally subdued Israel's enemies in the Promised Land, and he sat down before the nation on his throne in the capital of the Promised Land, Jerusalem. Many aspects of the next Feast on our calendar, Day of Atonement, (which in Hebrew is "Yom Kippur"), suggest this time in Israel's history.

Here is what the High Priest was instructed to do on the Day of Atonement:

Leviticus 16:7-10

Then he is to take the two goats and present them before the LORD at the entrance to the Tent of Meeting. He is to cast lots for the two goats— one lot for the LORD and the other for the scapegoat. Aaron shall bring the goat whose lot falls to the LORD and sacrifice it for a sin offering. But the goat chosen by lot as the scapegoat shall be presented alive before the LORD to be used for making atonement by sending it into the desert as a scapegoat.

Leviticus 16:29-30

This is to be a lasting ordinance for you: On the tenth day of the seventh month you must deny yourselves and not do any work— whether native-born or an alien living among you— because on this day atonement will be made for you, to cleanse you. Then, before the LORD, you will be clean from all your sins.

THE DAY OF ATONEMENT: REPENTING OF SIN

The Day of Atonement was, and still is, the most solemn day in the Jewish calendar. Jews often refer to it as simply, "The Day." It is a day of repentance and mourning when Jews fast and pray with great regret for the sins they've committed. On this day, Jews are instructed to afflict their souls in remorse for their transgressions.

Many of the distinctive aspects of the Day of Atonement revolve around two goats. On the day of the Feast, the High Priest would cast lots to determine which of the two goats was for the Lord, and which was for Azazel. ("Azazel" is thought to be an ancient name for God's enemy, Satan.) The goat for the Lord was slaughtered, and the blood of this goat gave the High Priest permission on this one day of the year to enter, on behalf of the people, the Holy of Holies where the Ark of the Covenant with its gold cherubim cover lay.

Over and over again, the Scriptures tell us that the Lord is enthroned between the cherubim on the Ark of the Covenant. (This style of throne room was not uncommon in the ancient Middle East.) The Bible says: "And they brought back the Ark of the Covenant of the Lord Almighty, who is enthroned between the cherubim (I Samuel 4:4)." "The Lord reigns, let the earth tremble; He sits enthroned between the cherubim, let the earth shake (Psalm 99:1)." The Ark, also called the Mercy Seat, was His throne seat. When the High Priest entered into the Holy of Holies the Day of Atonement, he was entering the very throne room of God on earth.

In the time of kings and kingdoms, no one could enter a throne room or approach the king's seat without permission. (The wonderful Old Testament book of Esther is the story of a beautiful Jewish queen who entered the throne room of Persia without permission. You must read this delightful short story to find out what happened!) When the High Priest entered the throne room of God in the Tabernacle, the permission God granted was through the blood of the goat that had been selected for Him.

Historians tell us that when the High Priest entered the throne room and stood before the Mercy Seat on the Day of Atonement each year, the other priests would tie a rope to his leg. They did this in case the High Priest had entered the throne room without executing all the Scriptural requirements. They knew that if the High Priest were in the throne room without permission, he was a gonner. And since the other priests didn't have permission to enter the throne room even to retrieve his dead body, they needed to be sure they had a way of getting him out!

Before the High Priest entered the Holy of Holies on behalf of the people, he would say to the congregation, "Blessed be the Name of His glorious Kingdom forever and ever." The people would respond,

"Blessed be the Name of His glorious Kingdom forever and ever." Then, while the High Priest was before the Mercy Seat throne, he would say a prayer derived from the book of Genesis, which is recorded in the Talmud: "May the scepter not depart from the House of Judah." On the Day of Atonement, the High Priest and the people were focused on a kingdom, and a king from the line of Judah.

THE DAY OF ATONEMENT: SUBDUING GOD'S ENEMIES

Meanwhile, the goat for Azazel was still outside. After the High Priest had completed his tasks in the Holy of Holies throne room, another priest would lay his hands on Azazel's goat. He would lay the blame for all the sins of the people on this goat, also called the "scapegoat." (That is why we call someone who takes the blame for something a scapegoat.) The priest would then lead the scapegoat out into the wilderness. He was not commanded to kill the goat, but to make sure that the goat with their sins laid on it didn't return to Jerusalem, the custom developed of throwing the goat off a cliff into an abyss.

THE DAY OF ATONEMENT AND DAVID'S REIGN

Does the Day of Atonement remind you of when the people solemnly mourned their sins during the time of repentance during David's reign? On the Day of Atonement, Jews are instructed to afflict their souls, and mourn for their sins (Leviticus 16). Could the Feast have been pointing the people's minds to the time during David's reign when, following his example, and using his songbook, the people would mourn their sinfulness and acknowledge their dependence on God?

Does the Day of Atonement remind you of the throne established for King David? When the priest entered God's throne room on the Feast, he would pray about a glorious kingdom, with a king from the line of Judah finally ruling the land that God had promised to Abraham. Could the Feast have been pointing to the Kingdom of David?

Does the Day of Atonement remind you of the removal of Israel's enemies from the Promised Land during David's reign? When the priest led the enemy Azazel's goat out of the community, he would throw it into an abyss. Could the Feast have been pointing to the time when King David would remove God's enemies from the Promised Land?

And could it be,
that just as God might have delivered the fall Feasts
to point ahead to a time
when the children of Israel would dwell in
the Promised Land,
that those Feasts might still point ahead to a time
when Jesus the Messiah will return to dwell in
the Promised Land?

AN EVERLASTING COVENANT WITH DAVID

When God had King David anointed, He made a mind-boggling covenant with David. He told David that he would have an "everlasting dynasty (II Samuel 7)." That kind of promise is hard to comprehend, because we know from the Bible that even the earth isn't even going to last forever, yet God promised King David that his throne would last forever. "Your house and your kingdom will endure forever before Me; your throne will be established forever (II Samuel 7:16)."

II Samuel 7:8-16

"Now then, tell My servant David, 'This is what the LORD Almighty says: I took you from the pasture and from following the flock to be ruler over My people Israel. I have been with you wherever you have gone, and I have cut off all your enemies from before you. Now I will make your name great, like the names of the greatest men of the earth. And I will provide a place for My people Israel and will plant them so that they can have a home of their own and no longer be disturbed. Wicked people will not oppress them anymore, as they did at the beginning and have done ever since the time I appointed leaders over My people Israel. I will also give you rest from all your enemies.

"'The LORD declares to you that the LORD Himself will establish a house for you: When your days are over and you rest with your fathers, I will raise up your offspring to succeed you, who will come from your own body, and I will establish his kingdom. He is the one who will build a house for My Name, and

I will establish the throne of his kingdom forever. I will be his father, and he will be My son. When he does wrong, I will punish him with the rod of men, with floggings inflicted by men. But My love will never be taken away from him, as I took it away from Saul, whom I removed from before you. Your house and your kingdom will endure forever before me; your throne will be established forever.'"

How could God possibly keep this promise to King David? How could one of David's descendants be sitting on David's throne, even after the earth passes away? Wouldn't David have to have a descendant who is eternal?

AN EVERLASTING DESCENDANT OF DAVID
The New Testament books of Matthew and Luke trace the lineage of Jesus the Messiah back to King David of the tribe of Judah. That's why Jesus is sometimes called the "Son of David," since the word "son" can also mean descendant (Matthew 9:27). Jesus, the eternal Son of God, is also a son of David. He is both God and man at the same time, and His manhood descended directly from King David. He was the eternal heir to the throne that was promised to King David in 1000 BC.

The Bible tells us that there is a time coming when Jesus will return to sit down on David's throne in Jerusalem. This time will come after Jesus returns for the Bride of Christ. Do you remember I told you that after a Jewish groom returned for his bride, he would spend seven days alone with her before he presented her to the assembly? After Jesus returns for His bride the Church, the Bible tells us that we will spend a period of time away from the earth with Jesus. The ninth chapter of the book of Daniel strongly suggests that this will be a seven-year period of time.

JESUS ON DAVID'S THRONE
But then the day will come when Jesus will present His bride to the earth, and will sit down on His (and David's) throne in Jerusalem. His bride will be permitted to enter the throne room by virtue of His blood. On that day, Jesus will defeat Israel's enemies in a mighty battle called Armageddon, and He will take Satan away and throw him into the abyss for one thousand years (Revelation 20:2-3). The people who will

have remained on earth will mourn their sin of rejecting the Son who was pierced on the cross for their transgressions. God says on that day, "They will look on Me whom they have pierced, and they will mourn Me as one mourns an only son (Zechariah 14:4)."

Revelation 20:2-3

He seized the dragon, that ancient serpent who is the Devil and Satan, and bound him for one thousand years. He threw him into the abyss, closed it, and put a seal on it so that he would no longer deceive the nations until the thousand years were completed.

Many Jews call the Day of Atonement by its Hebrew name, "Yom Kippur," or by its nickname, "The Feast of Face to Face." Those who belong to Jesus will indeed see Him face to face on His throne in Jerusalem. They will be there by virtue of the King's own blood, the permission required to enter the throne room. "They shall see His face (Revelation 22:4a)." But even those who have not been adopted as His sons will see Him on that day, and they will mourn.

In the Old Testament we learn that every fifty years, on the Day of Atonement, the Jubilee Year began (Leviticus 25:8-19). On this special Feast day, all debts in the land were forgiven, and all slaves were set free. It was a time for making all things right— to make a fresh start without the burden of debt or enslavement. It was like a clean slate.

When the Lord instituted the Day of Atonement, it seemed to point ahead to a time when a king would rule the Promised Land, God's enemies would be subdued, and His people would solemnly mourn their sins. The Feast continues to point us to a time when our Messiah King will rule from Jerusalem in the Promised Land, Satan will be subdued, and all the people left on earth will mourn their sins. The very special, twice-a-century Yom Kippur that begins the Jubilee year continues to hint at a time of a fresh start of freedom and prosperity for freed slaves.

Perhaps, just perhaps,
the event which the Feast has invoked,
year after year, century after century,
will occur on the actual day of the Feast!

HOW ABOUT YOU?

DO YOU EVER FEEL LIKE THE ISRAELITES? YOU TELL GOD YOU'RE SORRY FOR A SIN, YOU RESOLVE NOT TO DO IT AGAIN, THEN BEFORE YOU KNOW IT, YOU'RE CAUGHT UP IN THE SAME SIN AGAIN? THE APOSTLE PAUL IN THE NEW TESTAMENT HAD THE SAME PROBLEM. "I DO NOT UNDERSTAND WHAT I DO. FOR WHAT I WANT TO DO I DO NOT DO, BUT WHAT I HATE I DO (ROMANS 7:15)."

THE GREAT NEWS ABOUT YOUR FATHER IN HEAVEN IS THAT HIS MERCIES ARE NEW EACH MORNING. "BECAUSE OF THE LORD'S GREAT LOVE, WE ARE NOT CONSUMED, FOR HIS COMPASSIONS NEVER FAIL. THEY ARE NEW EVERY MORNING; GREAT IS YOUR FAITHFULNESS (LAMENTATIONS 3:22-23)."

YOU CAN NEVER TRAVEL SO FAR THAT YOU ARE BEYOND THE REACH OF HIS MERCY. YOU CAN NEVER SINK SO LOW THAT HE CAN'T LIFT YOU UP. YOU CAN NEVER OUT-SIN THE BLOOD OF JESUS.

IF YOU FEEL LIKE YOU'VE JUST MESSED UP TOO MANY TIMES, AND JESUS WOULD NEVER TAKE YOU BACK— THINK AGAIN. HE SAID, "MY FATHER, WHO HAS GIVEN THEM (THAT'S YOU!) TO ME IS GREATER THAN ALL; NO ONE CAN SNATCH THEM (THAT'S STILL YOU!) FROM MY FATHER'S HAND (JOHN 10:29)." IF YOU HAVE TRUSTED IN CHRIST, YOU HAVE BEEN GIVEN AS A GIFT FROM THE FATHER TO THE SON. AND JESUS WOULD NEVER CAST AWAY A GIFT HIS FATHER HAS GIVEN HIM!

IF YOU HAVE FALLEN INTO SIN, STOP IT. CONFESS YOUR SIN, AND RUN TO THE CROSS. YOU'LL FIND FORGIVENESS AND CLEANSING THERE, AND A FRESH SLATE. YOU'LL ALSO FIND THE POWER TO CONQUER YOUR SIN. IN FACT, GOD TELLS US THAT THE POWER HE GIVES HIS CHILDREN IS THE SAME POWER THAT RAISED JESUS' DEAD BODY FROM THE GRAVE (EPHESIANS 1:19-20). PRETTY POWERFUL, HUH?

GOD SAID THAT WHEN HE FORGIVES OUR SINS, HE REMEMBERS THEM NO MORE. IF GOD CAN'T REMEMBER YOUR SIN, YOUR SLATE IS REALLY CLEAN!

THE SEVENTH FEAST: TABERNACLES

"The Word became flesh and made His dwelling among us. We have seen His glory, the glory of the One and Only, who came from the Father, full of grace and truth (John 1:14)."

THE TABERNACLE

From the time of the Exodus all the way through King David's reign, God had allowed the manifestation of His glory to dwell among His people in the Ark of the Covenant. The Ark itself rested in a large tent called the "Tabernacle," or the "Tent of Meeting," or the "House of God." The Tabernacle was the most beautiful tent that ever there was.

Around the Tabernacle was an open "square," fifty feet long by seventy-five feet wide. (I know those aren't the dimensions of a square, but for some reason people still call it that.) Around it was a curtain of fine linen over seven feet high, in bright colors, hanging on posts of brass. At one end of the square, separated by a curtain, was the Court, where only the priests could enter. Within the court was the Tabernacle, a tent made not of cloth, but of removable wood panels covered in gold that stood upright on silver bases. The Tabernacle itself was divided by a veil into two rooms: the Holy Place, and the Holy of Holies. It was in the inner sanctum of the Holy of Holies that the Ark of the Covenant rested.

During the Israelites' forty years in the desert, when the pillar of cloud moved, everyone had to move with it, and the priests from the tribe of Levi were responsible for assembling and disassembling the tabernacle as they moved. All of the components of the tabernacle, including the Ark of the Covenant, were designed to be portable, just like a tent. When God moved in the pillar of cloud, the Levites got hopping and packed up the Tabernacle.

During the period of the Judges, the Tabernacle stayed most of the time in a town called Shiloh. There the priests performed the sacrifices and offerings that the Law required. Even though the Ark of the Covenant remained stationary most of the time, it continued to be housed in a portable tent.

A PERMANENT HOME FOR THE ARK OF THE COVENANT

When King David finally had rest from his enemies, and sat down on his throne, he decided he wanted to build a permanent home for the Ark of the Covenant. Since Israel was finally established in the land God had promised on oath that He would give them, and since the people had repented of their idol worship, David felt it was about time for the focus of the worship of the Lord to be in a beautiful, permanent building, and not just in a tent.

But God had a different plan. He told David that his son would be the one who would build a house for God's Name (II Samuel 7:13). Though I'm sure David was disappointed, he obeyed God, and prepared his son Solomon for the building of the Temple of the Lord, where the Ark of the Covenant would finally rest in the land God had promised.

And what a glorious temple David's son King Solomon built on top of Mount Moriah! The layout of the Temple was copied after that of the Tabernacle, except that it was larger, and made of stone and cedar. The Temple had two courts around it, both open to the sky, with walls of stone around them. The outer court was for the people, but the inner court was for the priests only, and it contained the altar upon which the offerings to God were made. Within the court of the priests stood the Holy House, where the High Priest and his sons lived. Within the Holy House was the Holy Place, where the table of showbread and the golden lampstand stood. And finally, within the Holy Place, was the Holy of Holies, where the Ark of the Covenant rested.

Solomon built a palace where he lived in state on the south slope of Mount Moriah, just below the Temple. It contained so many cedar pillars imported from Lebanon, that it was called "The House of the Forest of Lebanon." The palace included a regal throne room called the "Hall of Justice." Solomon built a wide stone stairway, connecting his palace to the Temple, so that he could go to the Temple to worship.

During Solomon's reign, Israel lived in peace, with enormous, secure borders. The cultural life of Israel flourished with exquisite literature, lovely music, and great gains in the study of zoology and botany. This era of peace and prosperity in the Promised Land is often referred to as the "Golden Age of Israel." It was the pinnacle of Israel's history, as the nation was the most powerful on earth at that time. People, including the Queen of Sheba from Ethiopia, would travel thousands of miles to see the riches of Solomon's kingdom, to hear the wisdom from his throne, and to worship at the magnificent Temple where the glory of Israel's God dwelt among men.

When God delivered the Feast of Tabernacles to Moses, it gave hints about a time 500 years in the future when a king would rule with peace and prosperity in the Promised Land, and God would "tabernacle" among His people. (The Bible actually uses the word "tabernacle" as a verb to describe God living among men!)

Leviticus 23:42-43

"Celebrate the Feast of Tabernacles for seven days after you have gathered the produce of your threshing floor and your winepress. Be joyful at your Feast— you, your sons and daughters, your menservants and maidservants, and the Levites, the aliens, the fatherless and the widows who live in your towns. For seven days celebrate the Feast to the LORD your God at the place the LORD will choose. For the LORD your God will bless you in all your harvest and in all the work of your hands, and your joy will be complete."

Deuteronomy 16:13-15

"Live in booths for seven days: All native-born Israelites are to live in booths so your descendants will know that I had the Israelites live in booths when I brought them out of Egypt. I am the LORD your God."

The Feast of Tabernacles is the most joyous Feast of Even today in Israel, people set up tents (also called b tabernacles), and decorate them with palm branches and fruits. They eat outdoors and celebrate with gladness for seven days. They give gifts to the poor, and share food with their neighbors. They are *commanded* to be joyful.

In the middle of the prosperous, peaceful reign of Solomon that the Feast of Tabernacles suggested, Solomon completed the Temple of the Lord. No longer would God tabernacle in the Tabernacle; He would dwell among men in a glorious Temple. Solomon dedicated the Temple *on* the Feast of Tabernacles, and I don't think he was prepared for what happened on that Feast day:

II Chronicles 7:1-3

When Solomon finished praying, fire came down from heaven and consumed the burnt offering and the sacrifices, and the glory of the Lord filled the temple. The priests could not enter the temple of the Lord because the glory of the Lord filled it. When all the Israelites saw the fire coming down and the glory of the Lord above the temple, they knelt on the pavement with their faces to the ground, and they worshiped and gave thanks to the Lord, saying, "He is good; His love endures forever."

Wow. The era to which the Feast of Tabernacles had hinted for 500 years commenced *on* the Feast of Tabernacles when Solomon dedicated the Temple. Now the throne room of God, the Holy of Holies, was housed in one of the Seven Wonders of the Ancient World, Solomon's Temple, connected by a stairway to the throne room of King David. At the dedication, God made His presence manifest in such a dramatic fashion that those gathered could do nothing but put their faces to the ground and worship. The priests couldn't even enter the Temple because of the glory of the Lord!

For centuries, the Feast of Tabernacles suggested a golden era of peace and prosperity in the Promised Land with God tabernacling among His people. Isn't it fascinating that the era was instituted *on* the Feast of Tabernacles during Solomon's reign?

And could it be,
that just as God might have delivered the fall Feasts
to point ahead to a time
when the children of Israel would dwell in
the Promised Land,
that those Feasts might still point ahead to a time
when Jesus the Messiah will return to dwell in
the Promised Land?

JESUS' FEAST OF TABERNACLES: WATER AND LIGHT

When Jesus lived on earth, the Feast of Tabernacles was celebrated at the Temple, where two very interesting traditions had been incorporated into the Feast. The first new tradition happened on the last and greatest day of the seven-day Feast, when the High Priest would conduct a "water libation ceremony." In it, he would take a pitcher full of water, drawn from the Spring of Gihon, where Solomon had been anointed king of Israel (I Kings 1:45). As the joyful assembly stood waving palm branches, shouting, "Raise your hand," he would raise the pitcher in his hand higher and higher, and then pour out the water. The second new tradition happened on that same day at dusk, when men would climb on ladders to light three seventy-five-foot high torches. As the flames blazed from these enormous torches, priests lit dozens of smaller torches, and jubilantly danced through the Temple courtyards. The light could be seen all over Jerusalem.

The book of John records a time when Jesus attended the Feast of Tabernacles on this special day of the Feast when water flowed and the Temple was full of light.

John 7:37-39

On the last and greatest day of the Feast, Jesus stood and said in a loud voice, "If anyone is thirsty, let him come to Me and drink. Whoever believes in Me, as the Scripture has said, streams of living water will flow from within him." By this He meant the Spirit, whom those who believed in Him were later to receive.

And later that same day,

John 8:12

When Jesus spoke again to the people, He said, "I am the light of the world. Whoever follows Me will never walk in darkness, but will have the light of life."

Jesus told the crowd assembled at the Temple that He was the source of Living Water, and that He was the Light of the World. We know that this is true at least in a metaphorical sense. Our souls thirst for God, and cannot be satisfied, except by God's Holy Spirit. People often attempt to slake their thirst by other, often sinful means, but they continue to languish with an unquenched thirst.

And Jesus truly is the light that we long for in our lives. His Word gives us direction when everything around us seems dark. He enables us see the world plainly, when others around us might seem confused and befuddled by the meaning of life. And a relationship with Jesus will brighten anyone's day.

JESUS' MILLENNIAL KINGDOM: WATER AND LIGHT

But could Jesus, on the Tabernacles Feast of Light and Water, possibly be pointing to something in the future? Could Jesus be telling us that water will literally come from Him, or that He will literally be light?

The Bible says that there is a time coming that will be similar in many ways to Solomon's reign. A joyful day is coming when there will be peace and prosperity on earth, when there will be rest from enemies, and when the Lord will tabernacle among His people. This new era is called the Millennial Kingdom.

Read what the Scriptures say about the Millennial Kingdom:

Revelation 22:1-5

Then the angel showed me the river of the water of life, as clear as crystal, flowing from the throne of God and of the Lamb down the middle of the great street of the city. On each side of the river stood the tree of life, bearing twelve crops of fruit, yielding its fruit every month. And the leaves of the tree are for the healing of the nations. No longer will there be any curse. The throne of

God and of the Lamb will be in the city, and His servants will serve Him. They will see His face, and His name will be on their foreheads. There will be no more night. They will not need the light of a lamp or the light of the sun, for the Lord God will give them light. And they will reign for ever and ever.

On the Feast of Tabernacles, as the water libation was being poured out, and Jesus, the Lamb, said, "Out of Me will come streams of living water," do you think He could have been giving us clues about the Millennial Kingdom where there will be a river of the water of life flowing from the throne of God?

And later on that Feast of Tabernacles, as the priests were lighting torches to set Jerusalem ablaze with light, when Jesus said, "I am the light of the world," could He have been giving us clues about the Millennial Kingdom when, "There will be no more night. They will not need the light of a lamp or of the sun, for the Lord God will give them light (Revelation 22:5)"?

THE KINGDOM OF GOD

Many Old Testament prophets wrote about a time in the future when God would return to tabernacle among His people, to sit down on the throne of David, and once again to fill Jerusalem with His glory.

Zechariah 8:3a
"I will return to Zion and will dwell in the midst of Jerusalem."

Amos 9:11
"I will restore the tabernacle of David."

Isaiah 4:5
Then the Lord will create over all of Mount Zion and over those who assemble there a cloud of smoke by day and a glow of flaming fire by night; over all the glory will be a canopy.

Jesus often referred to the Millennial Kingdom as the "Kingdom of God" or the "Kingdom of Heaven." It will last one thousand years while Satan is bound in the Abyss, and those who have faithfully followed Jesus will rule in the Kingdom with Him. The Messiah, Jesus, said, "I tell you the truth, at the renewal of all things, when the Son of Man sits on His glorious throne, you who have followed Me will also sit on twelve thrones, judging the twelve tribes of Israel (Matthew 19:28)." During Solomon's reign, the Temple with its throne room, and the Palace with its throne room were connected by a stairway on Mount Zion. A time is coming when those two throne rooms will again be connected, this time by the "canopy of God's glory."

What will it be like when Jesus returns to Jerusalem in His resurrection body, sends Satan to the Abyss for one thousand years, sits down on David's throne, is both light and water for the Kingdom, and rules in justice along with His faithful followers? I can hardly imagine. But the Scriptures give us some enticing glimpses of what is to come.

WHAT WILL THE MILLENNIAL KINGDOM BE LIKE?

For one thing, animals will become peaceful. In the Old Testament book of Isaiah, we read a famous passage about the Millennial Kingdom:

Isaiah 11:6-8

The wolf will live with the lamb, the leopard will lie down with the goat, the calf and the lion and the yearling together; and a little child will lead them. The cow will feed with the bear, their young will lie down together, and the lion will eat straw like the ox. The infant will play near the hole of the cobra, and the young child put his hand into the viper's nest.

Adults often think they're quoting this passage from the Bible when they say, "The lion will lie down with the lamb." But that's not in the Bible! If you've ever been bitten by a dog, or scared by a snake, you'll look forward to a time when all animals are tame. Do you think you'd like to have a pet panther, or have fun wrestling with a bear?

Just as in Solomon's kingdom, during the Millennial Kingdom, there will be no wars. The Old Testament writer Micah comforts God's people with these winsome words:

Micah 4:3

He will judge between many peoples and will settle disputes for strong nations far and wide. They will beat their swords into plowshares and their spears into pruning hooks. Nation will not take up sword against nation, nor will they train for war anymore.

That Bible quote is inscribed on the United Nations building in New York City. The United Nations say they want to do what Jesus *will* do when He reigns from His throne in the Kingdom. If your family has been devastated by the agony of losing a loved one in a war, you can appreciate how comforting this aspect of the Kingdom will be. During the Kingdom, when people have disagreements, they will not result in war. That will be a beautiful time.

In the Kingdom, everyone will acknowledge that Jesus is Lord, and all the earth will bow before Him. The apostle Paul tells us in the book of Philippians that there is coming a time when every knee will bow and every tongue will confess that Jesus Christ is Lord (Philippians 2:10-11).

The Scriptures tell us another thing about the Millennial Kingdom: the Feast of Tabernacles will be kept then! An Old Testament writer prophesied, "Then the survivors from all the nations that have attacked Jerusalem will go up year after year to worship the King, the Lord Almighty, and to celebrate the Feast of Tabernacles. If any of the peoples of the earth do not go up to Jerusalem to worship the King, the Lord Almighty, they will have no rain (Zechariah 14:16-7)."

John saw what was probably a vision of Feast of Tabernacles being kept in the Kingdom:

Revelation 7:9-10

After this I beheld, and, lo, a great multitude, which no man could number, of all nations, and kindred, and people, and tongues, stood before the throne, and before the Lamb, clothed with white robes, and palms in their hands; and cried with a loud voice, saying, "Salvation to our God, which sitteth upon the throne, and unto the Lamb."

Finally, I will describe one more thing that the Scriptures give us to look forward to in the Kingdom. Do you remember that I told you that after a Jewish groom made his betrothal-covenant, he would return to his father? Then, when the father said it was time, the groom would come at an hour the bride did not know, his friends would let out a shout and blow a trumpet, and he would snatch away his beloved. He would take her to be with him secluded in the bridal chamber for seven days. Then he would return to the community with his bride to show her off. Do you remember what I told you came next? There would be a wedding feast!

Well, the Bible tells us that the bride of Christ is now betrothed to Jesus. Jesus has returned to His Father, and we are waiting for the time when the Father says He can come with His angels, with a shout and a trumpet call, to snatch us away from the earth and to take us to the place He has prepared for us. We will remain there with Him for seven years, and then Jesus will return with us to show us to all those who remain on earth. Then, do you know what will happen? There will be a WEDDING FEAST! The Bible calls it the "Wedding Supper of the Lamb."

Revelation 19:7,9b

Let us rejoice and be glad and give Him glory! For the wedding of the Lamb has come, and His bride has made herself ready... Blessed are those who are invited to the Wedding Supper of the Lamb.

The Feast of Tabernacles recalls the Israelites' time in the wilderness, when they lived in peace, free from want, and God tabernacled with them— He in His Tabernacle, and they in theirs. It also hinted at the time in the Promised Land when His children would live in peace, free from want, when a son of David would sit on the throne, and God would tabernacle with them. And the Feast continues to suggest to us a time when all the world will live in peace, free from want, when *the* Son of David will sit on the throne, and God, wearing a tabernacle of flesh, will once again live among us.

Perhaps, just perhaps,
the event which the Feast has invoked,
year after year, century after century,
will occur on the actual day of the Feast!

HOW ABOUT YOU?

IF YOU'VE TRUSTED IN THE BLOOD OF THE LAMB OF GOD TO FORGIVE YOUR SINS, THE BIBLE SAYS THAT GOD HAS ADOPTED YOU INTO HIS FAMILY. IF A KING ADOPTS A SON, DO YOU KNOW WHAT HE BECOMES? A PRINCE! IF A KING ADOPTS A DAUGHTER, DO YOU KNOW WHAT SHE BECOMES? A PRINCESS! THINK ABOUT IT. IF THE KING OF ALL THE EARTH HAS ADOPTED YOU, YOU ARE A PRINCE OR A PRINCESS. I'M NOT TALKING ABOUT A FAIRY TALE PRINCE OR A DISNEY PRINCESS, BUT TRUE ROYALTY. THINK ELIZABETH I FIGHTING THE SPANISH ARMADA, OR HENRY V AT THE BATTLE OF AGINCOURT. STRONG. NOBLE. VALIANT.

IF GOD HAS ADOPTED YOU, NEVER FORGET WHAT THAT MAKES YOU: CHOSEN BY THE KING TO BE ROYAL. SINCE YOUR FATHER IS THE KING, YOUR SPEECH SHOULD BE EXCELLENT. SINCE YOUR FATHER IS THE KING, YOUR DRESS SHOULD BE RESPECTABLE. SINCE YOUR FATHER IS THE KING, YOUR BEHAVIOR SHOULD BE ABOVE REPROACH.

YOU DON'T SPEAK OR DRESS OR BEHAVE THIS WAY BECAUSE YOU HAVE TO; YOU DO IT BECAUSE OF WHO YOU ARE: NOBILITY! YOUR IDENTITY AS THE CHILD OF THE KING ELEVATES YOU SO THAT ONLY REFINED BEHAVIOR IS APPROPRIATE. CONDUCT YOURSELF WITH PROPRIETY, FOR THERE IS A CROWN UPON YOUR HEAD!

CONCLUSION

"The law is but a shadow of the good things that are coming— not the realities themselves (Hebrews 10:1)."

SHADOWS

Have you ever made a game of standing in front of a bright light, casting shadows on the wall? When you move, the shadow moves; when you freeze, the shadow freezes. The shadow has the form of your body, but of course none of the details, like the color of your eyes or the freckles on your face. It "approximates" you.

The Bible says that the law, in which we find all of the Feasts of the Lord, is but a shadow of the good things to come. Just like your shadow roughly depicts you, so the Feasts vaguely portray things that were and are to come.

The first four Feasts were shadows of things that Jesus did when He came to earth two thousand years ago. He suffered on the cross and died, bearing your sins and mine, being the perfect, eternal substitute that the Law required. After Jesus paid the penalty for our sins, He was buried, and lay in the grave. On the third day, however, He came back to life, and became the firstfruits of those who would come back from the grave. Fifty days later, the Feast of Pentecost marked His betrothal to His "bride" the church, and His promise to return for her.

The Bible tells us in the book in II Thessalonians chapter 4, that when Jesus returns for His bride, those who have trusted Him and are already dead will meet Jesus in the air first. Then, those who are still alive at His appearing will follow. Either way, if you've trusted in Him, you will meet the Lord in the air.

But what will it be like if you die *before* Jesus returns? I knew a boy named Jason who was walking to school one day, and was hit by a stray gang bullet; he died instantly. He didn't get to live to be 70 or 80; his life was snatched away in an instant, and yours might be too. Do you ever think about what will happen to you after you die?

Sometimes, when adults talk about what happens to us after we die, they get all muddle-headed in their theology. When a loved one dies, especially if her body had been ravaged by disease, they say, "Oh, Myrtle is in heaven now with a new body." Myrtle doesn't have her new body yet! Only Jesus, the Firstfruits from the dead has a new body right now.

PHASE I: PARADISE

When Jesus was hanging on the cross on that fateful Passover day, a criminal was hanging on a cross next to Him. The criminal said to Jesus, "Lord, remember me when You come into Your kingdom," and Jesus responded, "This day you shall be with Me in Paradise." The thief thought that Jesus was going to receive His kingdom right away, but Jesus knew better. That's probably why Jesus didn't say, "Yes, I'll remember you when I come into My kingdom," but rather, "This day you shall be with Me in *Paradise*." There is a phase of eternity, called "Paradise" that begins when a believer dies. (Later, a phase called "The Kingdom" begins. But that's later.)

If you have been adopted into God's family by faith in Jesus, and if you die before Jesus returns, then the moment you die you will be in Paradise. You won't have your resurrection body yet; not even Jesus had His resurrection body when He met the criminal from the cross in Paradise that Passover day. Jesus wouldn't get His resurrection body until two days later on the Feast of Firstfruits.

But Jesus' and the criminal's *souls* were going to be in Paradise together that Passover day. You can't touch or see your soul, but it's the part of you that reasons, and loves, and communicates with God. You can feel it inside you when you think or feel strong emotions. That's the part of you that will be instantly with Jesus in Paradise when you die. The Bible reassures us, "To be absent from the body is to be present with the Lord." For a believer, there is never a time when you're not with the Lord. You're either with Him with a body covering your soul, or you're with Him without a body covering your soul. Either way, He'll never leave you, nor forsake you. Death for a believer is like walking along and slinking off your coat as you're in mid-stride— except the coat is your body!

In the Old Testament, Paradise was called the "Bosom of Abraham," which conjures an image of safety and contentment. The Scriptures seem to indicate that Paradise will be a place to be reunited with loved ones who have died in the Lord. Two of my little babies died before they were born, and I look forward to Paradise when I can meet them for the first time.

But the part of Paradise that I'm most eagerly anticipating is SEEING JESUS. I know He'll be there, because He promised the criminal He would be. Whenever the glorified Jesus appeared to people in the Bible, they would drop to the ground, face in the dirt. I won't have my body yet, but I know my soul will do a drop-to-the-ground equivalent in His magnificent presence.

PHASE II: THE MILLENNIAL KINGDOM

But Paradise is just Phase I of what people generically refer to as "Heaven." Phase I will end when the Father says it is time for the Son, Jesus, to return to earth for His bride. When Jesus returns, the souls who have been in Paradise with Him will join Him, and Jesus will raise their dead bodies out of their graves and reconstitute them into resurrection bodies. Those bodies will be reunited with their souls, and at that point their redemptions will be complete! Body, mind and soul, all redeemed and restored to the way God intended them to be before sin entered the world.

After the souls who had been in Paradise with Jesus receive their resurrection bodies, then those believers who are alive when Jesus returns will receive theirs. Then, after Jesus conquers Israel's enemies and puts Satan into the Abyss, the Kingdom— Phase II— will finally begin.

At the beginning of the Kingdom, all believers will stand before the Judgment Seat of Christ. The Bible says, "We will all stand before the judgment seat of Christ, to give an account for the things done in the body (II Corinthians 5:10)." This is not a judgment to decide if you will go to heaven or hell. That is decided when you place your faith in Jesus. Jesus said, "I give them eternal life, and they shall never perish; no one can snatch them out of My hand. My Father, who has given them to Me is greater than all; no one can snatch them out of My Father's hand. My Father and I are one (John 10:28- 30)." If you have trusted Jesus, your eternal destination is sealed; your name is written in the Book of Life; you are in God's grip.

At the Judgment Seat, believers will receive rewards for their actions on earth. In discussing our behavior, the book of I Corinthians uses the metaphor of building a house. "If anyone builds on this foundation using gold, silver, costly stones, wood, hay or straw, his work will be shown for what it is, for the Day will bring it to light. It will be revealed with fire, and the fire will test the quality of each man's work (I Corinthians 3:12-13)." I don't know about you, but I want to be building on the foundation with gold, silver and costly stones. I don't want to spend my life living frivolously for my own pleasure, only to have it all burn up before my eyes at the judgment.

When I was a girl, there was nothing sweeter to my ears than to hear my father tell me that I had done a good job at something. At the Judgment Seat of Christ, Jesus will say to His obedient children, "Well done, good and faithful servant, enter into the rest of your Father (Matthew 25:21)." I think about that every day. Will He say that to me? Oh, I long to hear those words.

The other thing that thrilled me when I was a girl, was when my father gave me a reward for doing something especially good. Sometimes, for example, he would buy me an ice cream for having worked hard in the garden. Well, the Bible tells us that at the Judgment Seat, Jesus will give out REWARDS for good work. Jesus said in Revelation 22:12, "And behold, I am coming quickly, and My reward is with Me." Some people think it's unspiritual to be motivated by a reward. I don't. God is offering the reward so His children will want to glorify Him more. He tells us, "Run in such a way as to get the prize (I Corinthians 9:24b)." Receiving a prize from God motivated the apostle

Paul, who said, "I press on toward the goal to win the prize (Philippians 3:14)." Don't let anyone tell you Paul was unspiritual!

But the Judgment Seat is just the beginning of the Kingdom phase. During the one thousand-year long Kingdom, Jesus will be seated on David's throne in Jerusalem, and Jesus' faithful followers will rule with Him. Those who were faithful with much during their lives will be rewarded with the authority to rule over much. Those who were only a little faithful during their lives will have only a little authority.

When I was a child, I found nothing more appealing about adulthood than the idea of being in charge of things. I wanted to be the one to set rules and make plans, and not always to have decisions made for me. I wanted to have responsibility and authority. I looked forward to the day when I could tell someone to do something, and it would be done! I wanted finally to be the boss. Well, that's what the Kingdom will be like— only turbo-charged.

When you think about heaven, do you ever think that it might be just a little bit boring? Be honest. Do you ever picture opaque expressionless people, sitting on clouds playing really bad harp music forever and ever until they just want to pluck out their long white beards? Yuck! Get that picture out of your mind!

The Kingdom phase of heaven is going to be the most exciting, engaging time of your life! If you have been obedient to God and have served Him joyfully during your life on earth, then you're going to be in charge of things (Matthew 25-14-28). You'll be given authority, and people will have to answer to you. You'll have responsibilities and Jesus will be right there where you can see Him face to face.

And think about it: your rank in the Kingdom for one thousand years will be determined by how you behave on earth for only a few decades! Does that inspire you to go the extra mile for the Lord? Does that give you the motivation to live selflessly? Does that give you a reason to get out of bed each morning and scratch your head and think: What can I do today that will that will elevate my authority in the Kingdom for one thousand years?

PHASE III: THE ETERNAL STATE

If you've read this far, then I know you have a clever mind, and you're asking yourself, "Well, what happens after the thousand years?" The Bible says that at the end of the thousand years, the Lord will allow

Satan out of the Abyss, for just a little while. He then will finally put him into the Lake of Fire. That is a good and just punishment for the Lord's most vile and wicked enemy.

But here is my solemn and sober warning for you: The Lake of Fire is reserved for ALL of God's enemies. The Bible tells us that from our birth we are enemies of God. "Once you were alienated from God and were enemies in your minds because of your evil behavior (Colossians 1:21)." You were born God's enemy, and you will stay that way until you call on the name of the Lord to be saved. "If anyone's name was not found written in the Book of Life, he was thrown into the Lake of Fire (Revelation 20:15)."

If you haven't trusted Christ yet, your name is not written in the Book of Life. Don't wait and say that you'll do it tomorrow. Jesus, the Lamb of God, shed His blood for you on Passover. Apply His blood to the doorframe of your heart today by believing in Him. Jesus says, "Here I am! I stand at the door and knock. If any man hears My voice and opens the door I will come in and eat with him, and he with Me (Revelation 3:20)." Open the door of your heart and let Him in. The Bible says your eternal life begins when you know Him:

John 17:3

Now this is eternal life: that they may know You, the only true God, and Jesus Christ, whom You have sent.

Sometimes kids ask me, "How do I know if I've believed hard enough for Jesus to save me?" Here's the good news: It doesn't depend on how hard you've believed. Believing in Jesus for your salvation is like receiving an exquisitely wrapped gift. You hold out your hand and you take it! There's no worrying about whether you're good enough to receive it, or if you've held out your hand the right way to receive it. Jesus has offered you the gift, and you hold out your hand and take it. His Word says, "But the gift of God is eternal life through Jesus Christ our Lord (Romans 6:23b)."

Now, I know my clever readers are still asking, what happens next if you've received Jesus' exquisite free gift, you're no longer God's enemy, and you've served with responsibility in the Kingdom for one thousand years? Then what happens?

Well, the Bible doesn't give us a lot of specifics! Theologians call this next phase, Phase III, the "Eternal State." Sometimes I think that the Lord doesn't give us too many details about it because we just wouldn't get it. Perhaps the Lord will change the time-space continuum so that time doesn't exist anymore. Can you imagine life without time? I can't. God created time, and lives outside it. Perhaps in the Eternal State we will live outside time. I don't know.

Sometimes one of my little children will ask me a question like, "Why is the moon big sometimes, and little other times?" The real answer to that question involves lunar orbits, the earth's rotation, the location of the sun, and a little bit of calculus. But I usually just give a very simple answer like, "Well, we're moving and the moon is moving, so it always looks different to us." I can only give a little information, because that's all they can comprehend.

I think that's how is it with God's Eternal State, and our finite minds. We can only comprehend a little of what's coming, so God doesn't tell us much. But what He has told us is absolutely beautiful:

Revelation 21:4-5
He will wipe every tear from their eyes. There will be no more death, or mourning, or crying, or pain, for the old order of things has passed away. He who was seated on the throne said, "I am making everything new!" Then He said, "Write this down, for these words are trustworthy and true."

Let's go there together!

❊❊

END NOTES

1 The book of Genesis uses dates from the civil calendar; the book of Leviticus uses dates from the religious calendar. The seventh month of the civil calendar was the same as the first month of the religious calendar. That's how the seventeenth day of the seventh month mentioned in Genesis 8 can be – and in fact *is* – the very same date as the seventeenth of Nisan in Leviticus 23! The differences in the two dating systems are similar to those between our school year that begins in September and our calendar year that begins in January.

2 To understand the animal sacrifices of the Old Testament, think of them as charges on a credit card. Several times a month, I go to the supermarket, fill my cart with food, and then go to the cashier. Instead of paying her with cash, I present to her a little piece of plastic with the word VISA on it. Then, I walk away with all those groceries. We both know that the little piece of plastic has no intrinsic value— by itself it is worthless. But it represents the fact that a payment is coming. I owe a debt for the groceries, and the credit card covers my debt until a payment is made in the future. The grocer accepts the arrangement because he knows that a payment is coming. At the end of the month, money must go to VISA to fully pay for everything I bought with my credit card. Then the debt I owe the grocer is completely satisfied. My bill is marked, "Paid in full."

In the Old Testament, those who were waiting for Messiah knew that their sin required payment. God told them to offer animal sacrifices at the Temple, and those sacrifices would cover their debt temporarily, like my VISA card covered the groceries. But the Temple sacrifices couldn't pay the debt; they only covered the debt temporarily until the full payment came. Year in and year out, sin-charges were made to the account, and God accepted the animal sacrifices because He knew that the perfect payment-in-full sacrifice was coming. That perfect sacrifice was the sinless body of Jesus. Do you remember what Jesus said on the cross? "Tetelestai." *Paid in full.* All those animal sacrifice "credit card charges" covering the sins of the people year-in and year-out were paid in full, with a check signed in blood by Jesus Christ— the blood He shed on the cross.

3 You might wonder how the people knew that they could believe someone who claimed to be a prophet and was speaking for God. How would a person know that someone wasn't just making up lies and saying that they were from God? God wanted His children to understand His will without having to guess. In order that we may know the truth, God permitted His prophets to do miracles— things that could be done only by the power of God. Moses proclaimed, "The Lord says, 'Let My people go,'" then he parted the Red Sea. Elijah said, "Let it be known this day that You are God in Israel, and that I am Your servant, and that I have done all these things at Your word." Then he brought down fire from heaven (I Kings 18:37-38). I'd say that's corroborating evidence! The miracles authenticated the prophets' authority to say what they did. If they hadn't been speaking for God, they never would have been able to do those miracles.

4 The sacred Jewish text the *Mishnah* identifies Sivan 6, the date of the Feast of Weeks, as the time of the Tower of Babel story from Genesis 11. In that story we learn that after Noah's flood, all the people of the earth spoke one language. Despite the fact that God had told them to spread out over all the earth, the people had chosen to remain together, and to build a tower to reach the heavens. To correct them, the Lord came down and confused their language, so that they could not understand one another's speech.

Isn't it fascinating that the date the Jews have always identified with the confusion of the languages of the earth was also the date of Pentecost, when people who had been confused by other languages could all of a sudden comprehend them? The curse of Babel was reversed on Pentecost, and the two events are believed to share the same anniversary. Amazing!

Made in the USA
San Bernardino, CA
05 December 2013